WOMEN
THROUGH THE
BIBLE

• *Marlys Taege* •

WOMEN
THROUGH THE
BIBLE

Devotions for Women's Groups

CPH.
SAINT LOUIS

Copyright © 1987 Concordia Publishing House
3558 S. Jefferson Avenue, St. Louis, MO 63118-3968
Manufactured in the United States of America

Library of Congress Cataloging in Publication Data

Taege, Marlys, 1928-
    Women through the Bible.

    1. Women in the Bible—Meditations. 2. Women—Prayer-books and devotions—English. I. Title.
BS575.T34 1987   242'.643   87-17593
ISBN 0-570-04460-X

6 7 8 9 10 11 12 13 14 15   07 06 05 04 03 02 01 00 99

To my family, especially my father,
Daniel A. Schmidt,
and my sainted mother,
L. Irene Hoy Schmidt,
whose sacrifices and support
enabled me to obtain an education
and pursue a career in
Christian journalism.
Special thanks to my son-in-law,
Marshall Beale,
for his interest in this manuscript
and for his help in proofreading.

Contents

Preface
.... 9

Old Testament
Beginnings: Don't Say, "Never!"
    Genesis 11
Power of God: And Sarah Laughed
    Genesis 14
The Value of Life: I'm So Glad I'm Me!
    Exodus 17
Worship and Praise: And Miriam Led the Women
    Exodus 20
Purification: Beyond All That Blood Stuff?
    Leviticus 23
Inheritance: A Request from Five Daughters
    Numbers 26
Blessings of the Law: Choose Life!
    Deuteronomy 29
Prayer: Praying Is Believing
    Joshua 32
Leadership: When the Lord Taps You on the Shoulder
    Judges 35
Family of God: Your People Will Be My People
    Ruth 38
Wisdom: Common Sense Plus!
    1 and 2 Samuel 41
Hospitality: The Bowl Did Not Run Out
    1 and 2 Kings 44
Building: The Lord Knows!
    1 Chronicles 47
Prophecy: In the Footsteps of Huldah
    2 Chronicles 50
Family Unity: Opposites Attract!
    Ezra 53
Perseverance: Tough on the Outside—Sweet on the Inside
    Nehemiah 56

Principles: If I Must Die
Esther 58
Problems/Blessings: Twice Blest!
Job 61
Sing: Make a Joyful Noise unto the Lord!
Psalms 64
Priorities: She Speaks with Gentle Wisdom
Proverbs 67
True Love: No Wonder All Women Love You!
Ecclesiastes/Song of Solomon 70
Compassion: My Love for You Will Never End
Isaiah 73
Judgment: No "Put-Downs"
Jeremiah—Ezekiel 75
The Prophets: I Want Your Love!
Daniel—Malachi 78

New Testament

Evangelism: I Have Good News!
Matthew 81
Worry: Don't Be Afraid
Mark 84
Generosity: She Gave All She Had
Mark 87
Trust: No One Told the Neighbors
Luke 90
Bible Study: Letter from the Lord
Luke 93
The Trinity: Three-in-One—the Total God
Luke 96
Home Missions: I Want to Go to Africa
John 99
Faith: I Believe
John 101
Talents: God Doesn't Do a Bum Job
Acts 103
Careers: Profits Doubled
Acts 106

8

Christian Service: Strengthen One Another
Romans 109
Orderliness: Friday Was Cleaning Day
1 and 2 Corinthians 112
Freedom: Free to Be Me
Galatians 115
Marriage: Submit Yourselves to One Another
Ephesians 118
Unity: Dealing with Differences Differently
Philippians 121
Understanding: Give an Answer!
Colossians 124
Work: That's Success!
1 and 2 Thessalonians 127
Christian Homes: We Grandmother You!
1 and 2 Timothy 130
Self-control: They're Acting Like Children!
Titus/Philemon 133
Peace: The Unaccepted Gift
Hebrews 136
Neighbors: Friends—or Strangers?
James 139
Gifts: Decisions, Decisions!
James 142
Ageless Beauty: Insured but Sure to Disappear
1 and 2 Peter/1, 2, 3 John/Jude 145
Heaven: The Bride of Christ
Revelation 148

Conclusion
In Conclusion: Rejoice
.... 151

Notes
.... 155

Preface

To help "break the ice" at a zone meeting of a churchwomen's organization a few years ago, the pastoral counselor devised a contest. He divided the women into two groups and asked one to name women of the Bible and the other to name Biblical men. Because the pastor didn't believe the group naming women would know enough women in the Bible to win, he slipped that side a "crib sheet." With the aid of his list, the side naming women won!

Perhaps because of that experience, two questions came immediately to mind when I was asked to do a book of devotions for women.

The first question: How many of us women have ever really read the Bible—not *studied* but *read* it? Ever since childhood, I have been acquainted with God's Word through Sunday school lessons, confirmation class, adult Bible study, and regular church attendance, but until this assignment, I had never really read the Scriptures as a book, all the way through from cover to cover.

How many others have missed the full impact of God's activity in this world through helter-skelter Bible reading, I wondered. How many have assumed from the word by word, verse by verse approach of most study groups that normal reading of God's Word would be unproductive or uninteresting? How many have been deterred by the lists of "begats" and the unfamiliar names? Or how many have done the chapter-here-chapter-there approach outlined in numerous through-the-Bible study guides but never read the chapters of the Bible in sequence?

Encouraging women to read the entire Bible—and helping them enjoy it—became one goal of this devotional series.

My second question was: What does the Bible really say to and about women? Some years ago members of a Lutheran Church—Missouri Synod Task Force on Women began their deliberations by reading the four gospels from that perspective. They were excited by the multitude of references to women and the encouraging messages for women which they discovered!

Would the same thing happen if one approached the entire Bible in the same way, I wondered. I decided to find out. I began reading, and this book is the result.

As I read, I tried to place myself in the time span of each book. I tried to walk in the sandals of the faithful women I met. Each became a personal friend, rather than a character in an ancient but true story.

I found myself on a spiritual "high" for weeks as the power, the love, and the justice of our Lord, especially in the less familiar Old Testament accounts, became more apparent and more understandable than ever before in my life. In the New Testament, beloved passages took on new meanings for me as a woman when viewed from the broad brush-stroke perspective of *all* of God's Word.

Now my prayer is that these devotions will encourage you to read the Bible from Genesis to Revelation—to read it with joy and to discover with delight just how much our marvelous triune God cares about women as individuals, as persons with potential.

By using the devotions at monthly auxiliary meetings, members may be motivated to read the corresponding book(s) in the interim and thus cover the Bible in four years. By using one each week at home, along with the appropriate Scripture, members could finish the Bible in a year. Or, using the table of contents, a Christian growth chairman can find devotions related to a wide variety of program topics.

Whatever the use, the goal is the same: to help women grow spiritually and be assured that our loving Lord wants us to enjoy abundant life now and to live with Him forever in eternity.

Marlys Taege

Beginnings

Don't Say, "Never!"

F ew words are as exciting or hope-filled as the words "begin" or "beginning"—and few are as frightening. So as we begin our study of women in the Bible, let's think for a minute about a woman whose life was one new experience after another, a series of firsts, an adventure in the unknown. The woman is Eve, and her story is told in Genesis, the book of beginnings.

Imagine now that you are this first woman on earth. Do you find it difficult to identify with her? Can you imagine yourself walking in unclothed innocence through a sunny garden, picking fruit and nuts when you are hungry, seeing and personally knowing God, having no childhood memories, conversing with a snake, using leaves to fashion clothing for yourself and your husband, being the first woman to give birth to a baby (without the support of doctor or nurse, mother, sister, friend, or neighbor), wearing furs designed by the Lord, and then living to be hundreds of years old?

Perhaps, given our human history of fighting and famine, sickness and scandal, poverty and perversion, it's easier to identify with other events of Eve's life . . . her disobeying of God's command, the death of her second son at the hands of her firstborn, and her banishment from Eden.

But praise the Lord! Through it all, He's there—guiding and encouraging, teaching and correcting, sorrowing yet loving. Yes, God's with us today too. He created us, and He continues to care—that's the message of Genesis.

And what an amazing book it is, with all the firsts recorded there: the creation of the world in just seven days; the start of the human race, with its tremendous growth and longevity (Methuselah lived to be 969 years old!); the origin of the Sabbath and later the first sacrifices to the Lord; the first marriage; the beginning of poetry, cities, and music; the first judgment of God upon a sinful world through the greatest flood in history; the establishment of the chosen race of Israel, with leaders like Abraham, Isaac, and Jacob; and . . . the origin of sin!

Can you imagine how disappointed our Lord must have felt when Adam and Eve, His crowning creation, succumbed to the wiles of Satan instead of following their loving Father's directive? Nevertheless, He did not disown them—or us—but instead announced the best of all firsts: the first promise of a Savior.

Because of that Savior, we have hope. Because of that Savior, we can move boldly forward with new plans and new goals. In fact, as Rosa Parks told a 1984 breakfast meeting in Detroit, "This generation is as good as any to achieve our goals."

Do you remember Rosa? She was the tired black woman who calmly and politely refused to give a white man her seat on a Birmingham bus in December 1955. That act of courage led to her arrest, the loss of her job as a seamstress, and the beginning of the yearlong black boycott of Birmingham busses, which earned Rosa the title "Mother of the Civil Rights Movement in America."

She told that international audience in Detroit: Don't say "never" or "it won't happen in our lifetime." She's right, and the proof is in the amazing firsts of our century: frozen food, antibiotics, microwave cooking, no-iron fabrics, television, cars, jet planes, computers, laser surgery, and people on the moon, to mention just a few. Not since Eve has one generation seen more changes.

Our challenge now is to use these discoveries courageously for God-pleasing purposes, knowing that He will strengthen us for the task just as He did Eve and Rosa and all the women who have made new beginnings in His name over the centuries.

LET'S PRAY: Dear Lord, we begin our work/meeting/year in Your name, trusting in You to be with us. Guide us so that all we do will bring You glory and benefit Your people. In Jesus' name. Amen.

Power of God

And Sarah Laughed!

C reate the world in seven days? Our minds say it's impossible.

Make a human being from the soil of the earth? Unbelievable!

Separate the waters of the Red Sea long enough for all of God's chosen people to walk through? Improbable.

A man wrestling with the Lord and winning? Unlikely!

Two cities destroyed because of immorality—and a woman turned into a pillar of salt? Ridiculous.

Yes, the world laughs at the Biblical account of history, not understanding that with the Lord nothing is impossible. Even for Christians, the power of God is beyond our comprehension.

It was for Sarah, too.

As we read her story in Genesis, we find three visitors approaching the tent of Sarah and her husband, Abraham. Immediately Abraham extends the welcome mat, and Sarah prepares fresh bread, tender veal, milk and cream for them, even though it is mid-day, a time of rest in that hot climate.

After the meal, one of the visitors tells Abraham, "Nine months from now I will return, and Sarah will have a son" (18:14). Listening behind the door of the tent, an incredulous Sarah laughs. Her husband is 99 years old, and she is 90! She has long since given up hope for the blessing of a child and has encouraged her husband to sleep with her slave girl, Hagar. Hagar has conceived and given birth to Ishmael. Surely that is how Abraham's line will be continued.

The visitor hears Sarah laugh and asks her why.

It's then she realizes this guest is the Lord, and she is filled with fear. She denies that she laughed, but the Lord knows otherwise and again He says, "You laughed" (18:15).

Yes, this guest knows. He knows the present and the future, for He controls it. What He promises happens; what He wills is bound to be.

Imagine the awe of this childless woman as her husband is told, "Your descendants will become a great and mighty nation, through whom all the nations of the earth will be blessed."

And it happens as the Lord promises. In the remainder of Genesis, we learn the fascinating story of Abraham and Sarah's son, Isaac; his sons, Jacob and Esau; and Jacob's 12 sons, the progenitors of the 12 tribes of Israel.

It's the story of a Lord who cares and forgives and guides—and whose power is incomprehensible. Only today with modern microscopes and telescopes have we begun to fathom the complexity of this world which He created and the human mind and body which He formed in His image. If only the discovery of the billions of stars and planets, the exploration of outer space, and the power of the atom and the laser might lead all people to appreciate the limitless power of God, our Creator!

Not only is He all-knowing, all-powerful, and everywhere present, but wonder of wonders, this magnificent God created *us* to be His friends—not His robots, not His slaves, but His friends. Then to top it off, He gave us freedom of choice. (Perhaps you are laughing now in amazement—for you know the result.)

But God's ways are not our ways, and His most amazing characteristic is His unending love. It's that love that led Him to share His greatest gift, His only Son, our Savior.

What a God! What a Creator! What a Friend!

LET'S PRAY: Almighty God, we don't understand Your power, and we are astounded by Your love, but we are grateful for who You are and what You are.

Forgive our doubts, our disobedience, and our foolish laughter—and help us grow in faith and walk in Your ways. In Jesus' name. Amen.

The Value of Life

I'm So Glad I'm Me!

"And who are you?" an elderly woman asked a toddler at a family reunion. "I'm me!" the youngster responded with a happy smile.

Someone has incorporated that kind of joyous self-confidence into new words for the old tune "Ten Little Indians":

> (*Sing*) "I'm unique and unrepeatable.
> I'm unique and unrepeatable.
> I'm unique and unrepeatable.
> I'm so glad I'm me!"

We *should* be glad we're who we are, because each of us is the creation of the almighty God. Speaking to the Lord, David in Psalm 139 says, "You created every part of me; You put me together in my mother's womb." And, as Luther explains, God "has given me my body and soul, eyes, ears, and all my members, my reason and all my senses, and still preserves them." He even knows the number of hairs on our heads!

Yes, we are made by the Lord, and we are placed here for a purpose—for good works which He had in mind for us even before we were born (Eph. 2:10). What value that gives to human life . . . *each* human life, even the unborn and the newly born.

The story of Shiphrah and Puah illustrates this truth. We meet these two Egyptian midwives in Exodus, some years after Joseph had died. By this time the Israelites had multiplied to the point where they outnumbered the Egyptians. To keep them from becoming even more numerous, "the Egyptians put slave drivers over them to crush their spirits with hard labor" (1:11).

The king also told Shiphrah and Puah, "When you

help the Hebrew women give birth, . . . kill the baby if it is a boy, but if it is a girl, let it live" (1:16). However, these God-fearing women disobeyed the king. They let the boys live, and God blessed them for this.

Throughout the Book of Exodus, God shows similar concern for people—for human life—in other ways, too. After saving Moses from death as an infant and giving him miraculous powers as an adult, God sends not only Moses but also Aaron and Miriam to lead His people (Micah 6:4).

He frees them from slavery, personally guiding them out of Egypt with a pillar of cloud by day and a pillar of fire by night, even parting the waters of the Red Sea long enough to give all the Israelite men and their families an escape route. He sends manna and quails for food in the desert. He gives them moral and religious laws to assure their continued well-being. These laws include protecting widows and virgins (22:16, 22) and honoring mothers as well as fathers.

By contrast, what little respect we have for life today! Newspapers regularly carry stories of rape, murder, and child abuse. "Mercy killing" of the aged is gaining acceptance, and we permit hundreds of thousands of abortions each year.

We also sanction infanticide. In hospitals dedicated to saving lives, we withhold food and water from newborns who aren't perfect so that they will starve to death. In fact, a pediatric surgeon has developed a mathematical formula for determining which handicapped infants should live and which should die. Someone else has suggested that no baby should be considered a human being until the age of one month, and no birth certificate should be issued until then.

Failure to respect the sanctity of life has implications for all of us because no one is perfect. As Dr. Paul Bruch reminds us, when "someone starts drawing up a list of people who aren't perfect enough to live, watch out, because somewhere, way down on the list, you'll find your own name."[1]

How thankful we should be that the Lord's methods aren't the same as ours! He preserves life—and that includes our life, yours and mine. Knowing this and trusting in Him, can we do less for others?

LET'S PRAY: Dear Lord, thank You for making us who we are. Help us treasure and speak up for *life,* because all life is given by You for a purpose. In Jesus' name. Amen.

Worship and Praise

And Miriam Led the Women

Who is God to you?

- a Santa Claus who gives you gifts
- a judge who determines your guilt or innocence
- a teacher whose Word instructs you
- a parent who created and raised you
- a mind reader who knows your every thought
- a policeman who enforces laws
- a distant deity whose power inspires awe
- a loving friend who listens and cares about you
- a Savior who opens the door to eternal life

How we view God determines how we worship Him—joyfully, fearfully, thankfully, trustingly, reverently, willingly, grudgingly, regularly, or occasionally.

Certainly, our worship habits today stand in stark contrast to the exuberant praise offered in the days of the Exodus—and yet there are striking similarities. Sometimes the Hebrews doubted and complained and worshiped false gods, just as we do. More often, though, their relationship to the Lord was a personal one. God personally directed their escape from Egyptian bondage. He led them in their wilderness wanderings by means of a pillar of cloud by day and a pillar of fire at night.

God spoke directly with Moses, whose face shone as a result, causing the people to be afraid to go near Moses. Seventy leaders of Israel also "went up the mountain and . . . saw the God of Israel. Beneath His feet was what looked like a pavement of sapphire, as blue as the sky. . . . they saw God, and then they ate and drank together" (24:9-11). Later God told Moses that the people must "make a sacred Tent for me, so that I may live among them" (25:8).

Were the people grateful for this new place of worship and for the presence and guidance of the Lord over the years? Yes, as long as they had a strong human leader.

During the period covered in the Book of Exodus, God gave them a trio of leaders—Moses, Aaron, and their sister, Miriam, the prophetess. But only Moses was able to keep them in line. When Moses was on Mount Sinai receiving the Ten Commandments, the people felt forsaken and created a golden idol to worship.

That seems amazing, doesn't it, considering all the Lord had done personally for His people? What miracles He had enabled Moses to perform for their benefit! To persuade the Egyptian king to let them go, the Lord sent 10 plagues. Through Moses, He turned the waters of the Nile River into blood; covered the country with frogs and later with flies, gnats, and locusts; killed all the animals of the Egyptians; inflicted boils on the people; sent the worst hailstorm in Egyptian history; covered Egypt with darkness for three days—and finally, He killed all the firstborn of the Egyptians.

Is it any wonder then that after the Israelites' exciting escape through the Red Sea, Miriam took her tambourine and led the women in songs and dances of praise to God? Or that the Hebrews built altars to God throughout the countryside as they wandered in the wilderness? They knew Him as Creator, Protector, Rescuer, and Guide.

We too build churches wherever we settle, but today's believers worship the Lord more formally in liturgical formats that have come down to us through the years. Usually we reserve our cheers for sports heroes, our applause for stage performers, and our joy for leisure pursuits. We return from the Lord's Table with sad and solemn faces—even though our sins have just been forgiven. We forget that forgiven means *freed,* just as the Israelites were freed from the Egyptians. Yes, in Christ—in our great God—we are free!

Perhaps it's time to remember that "enthusiasm" comes from "en theos," two Greek words which mean "in God." Perhaps it's time to follow the example of Miriam; for surely, the Lord has done marvelous things for us, too!

LET'S PRAY: Almighty and all-loving God, we praise and thank You for the many blessings You have showered on us! We are so grateful for Your love and protection as we go about our daily work.May all that we do be accomplished ENTHUSIASTICALLY—in Jesus' name! Amen!

Purification

Beyond All That Blood Stuff?

A n evolutionist who was leading a nondenomina- tional Bible study was extoling the progress made by human beings since creation. People are growing kinder and more compassionate toward others and more concerned about their environment, she asserted. She spoke glowingly and longingly about the day when the church would evolve into a community totally united in Christian love, and people would know true peace.

"But," said a class member, "the beauty of being a Christian is that, despite our sins and mistakes, we can have that peace right now through faith in Christ Jesus. Through the shedding of His blood on the cross, we are washed clean . . . we're free!"

"Oh," responded the leader disparagingly, "I thought we were beyond all that blood stuff!"

Blood has long had negative connotations for many people—including women in Bible times, for whom it signified uncleanness. But a blood transfusion can re- store life, and blood in the Scriptures signifies life.

We find both concepts in Leviticus. This book is a manual or handbook for the Levites, the tribe assigned to protect and care for the tabernacle and to serve as priests. The book outlines the festivals the Israelites were to observe, the sacrifices they were to offer, and the laws of holiness and rites of purification they were to follow.

The sacrifices required of the Hebrews were pre- views or symbols of the salvation that is ours through Christ. As sinners, all human beings are under sen- tence of death, but God is willing to accept a substitute—another life for our life. How thankful we should be!

When the Hebrews sacrificed a lamb, goat, bull, or pigeon, it was to be perfect, just as Christ is perfect. As the penitent person put his hand on the living sacrifice, the believer's sin was transferred to the substitute, which was killed in his stead.

The Jews were forbidden to eat any blood because "life is in the blood"—and life belongs to God. It is His gift to us. For this reason, specific directives are given in Leviticus about what was to be done with the blood of the animals during the sacrifice.

Rules for offerings were numerous, too. They covered the burnt offering, a token of total dedication because it was totally consumed by the fire; the peace offering, a freewill gift of gratitude; the cereal or fellowship offering; and the sin and guilt offerings for unknown or unintended sins.

God gave these rules for one purpose: "You shall be holy and belong only to Me, because I am the Lord and I am holy. I have set you apart from the other nations so that you would belong to Me alone" (20:26).

God also set His people apart through the dietary laws which He gave for their health—and through the rites of purification. Any hemorrhaging or issue of blood, including menstruation and blood at childbirth, made a woman unclean. As a result, any bed on which she lay and anything on which she sat during this time was unclean. Anyone who touched an unclean woman had to wash his clothes and take a bath.

After her flow stopped, the woman was still unclean for seven days. For the ritual of purification on the eighth day, she had to take two doves or two pigeons to the priest, who would offer one as a sin offering and the other as a burnt offering. God's goal was not to demean women but to remind His people that they were born in sin and that pagan fertility rites and temple prostitution were not to be a part of their worship.

Against this background, we recall the New Testament woman who had an issue of blood for 12 years.

Imagine how she must have suffered. Then in faith, she touched Christ and was healed. But He didn't let it end there. "Who touched me?" He asked, seeking her out. "Your faith has made you whole," He told her when He found her—and our faith does the same for us.

What gratitude women owe to Christ for fulfilling those Old Testament laws. Through His love, we are purified. Through Him, we are clean and free to serve!

LET'S PRAY: Dear Father, we praise You and we thank You for purifying us for Your work through our faith in Jesus Christ. Amen.

26

Inheritance

A Request from Five Daughters

"You can't take it with you!" Despite the obvious truth of that adage, a few people have tried to prove it wrong. An eccentric millionaire asked to be buried in her expensive car, and the kings and queens of Egypt spent their lifetime constructing and stocking their pyramid tombs.

Although you can't take it with you, you can determine who receives the material blessings of your lifetime. Minnie spent her entire life doing just that. At every family gathering, she reminded family members of which dishes, which furniture, and which bank account each would receive when she died. And it happened—as she wished—because she had made a will.

Most Americans aren't so thorough. Experts estimate that 50 to 70 percent of U.S. adults have no will. For those persons, the state has made a "will." Unfortunately, these laws of intestacy may not satisfy the desires of the deceased or the survivors.

In the Book of Numbers, the daughters of Zelophehad didn't like the way the laws of Israel provided for distribution of property in their day either.

Numbers is in part what its name implies: a book of numbers. It records two censuses—one taken before the departure of the Israelites from Mount Sinai and the second taken 40 years later when they were preparing to enter the Promised Land of Canaan.

But Numbers is far more than a book of statistics; it's the story of the Israelites' life in the wilderness. Can you imagine 40 years of packing and unpacking . . . 40 years of having no permanent home . . . 40 years of dependence on the Lord for food and sometimes for water?

The Israelites were as sinful as we are. They often became discouraged and failed to trust in the Lord as they should. It was for this reason—in punishment for their lack of faith—that they were forced to wander in the wilderness for so long and only two of the original heads of families were allowed to enter Canaan. Even Moses displeased the Lord and was permitted only to view the Promised Land from a nearby mountain.

The first tribes to be settled were those with a large number of cattle: Gad, Reuben, and half the tribe of Manasseh. They liked the area east of the Jordan River, and God gave it to them before the others entered the Promised Land.

Among the latter tribe was the family of Zelophehad, the great, great, great-grandson of Joseph. He had no sons, but the Lord gave him five daughters: Mahlah, Noah, Hoglah, Milcah, and Tirzah.

After Zelophehad's death, the daughters became upset because women could not inherit property. Therefore this courageous female quintet went to the entrance of the tabernacle (the tent of the Lord's presence) and pleaded their case publicly. Speaking to Moses, Eleazar the priest, the tribal leaders, and the whole community, they said, "Just because he had no sons, why should our father's name disappear from Israel? Give us property among our father's relatives" (27:4).

When Moses presented their request to the Lord, the Lord agreed that they were right. He said, "Give them property among their father's relatives. Let his inheritance pass on to them. Tell the people of Israel that whenever a man dies without leaving a son, his daughter is to inherit his property" (27:7-8).

In the New Testament, God assures women of an even greater inheritance—life eternal through faith in Christ. Although the bishops of the early church at one time debated the question, "Does woman possess a soul?" the Lord assures us in Galatians 3:28 that "there is no difference . . . between men and women; you are all one in union with Christ Jesus."

That's the only inheritance that really matters—

and that fact disproves that old adage, for there *is* one thing in this life that you can take with you: your faith in God's Son, our Savior.

LET'S PRAY: Dear Lord, thank You for our homes and our possessions—and for the one inheritance that really matters, the gift of the Savior. Through faith in Him, we look forward to life eternal with You. In Jesus' name. Amen.

Blessings
of the Law

Choose Life!

*I*n Hawaii, it's against the law for people to put pennies in their ears. Dueling with water pistols is illegal in Massachusetts, and Maine forbids whistling on Sunday.[1] Even stranger regulations than these could undoubtedly be found if one were to examine the laws of most U.S. communities today.

If we look at Deuteronomy, the law book of the Hebrews, we can also find some regulations that on the surface seem strange. For instance:

• "Sew tassels on the four corners of your clothes" (22:12), and

• "When you build a new house, be sure to put a railing around the edge of the roof" (22:8).

Then there are laws which we might wish applied today: "When a man is newly married, he is not to be drafted into military service or any other public duty; he is to be excused from duty for one year, so that he can stay home and make his wife happy" (24:5).

Deuteronomy, which literally means "the second giving of the law," is a series of addresses by Moses to the 12 tribes of Israel as they prepared to enter the Promised Land. Knowing that he was going to die soon, Moses restated God's laws and commandments and reminded the people of the Lord's mercies and promises to them since they had left Egypt.

"Never forget these commands," Moses urged. "Teach them to your children. Repeat them when you are at home and when you are away, when you are resting and when you are working. Tie them on your arms and wear them on your foreheads as a reminder. Write them on the doorposts of your houses and on your gates" (6:6-9).

Why such an emphasis on the Law? Because God promised the Hebrews that all who kept His law would prosper and be blessed in everything they did (28:6). "I am now giving you the choice between life and death," God said. "Choose life. Love the Lord your God, obey Him and be faithful to Him, and then you and your descendants will live long . . . " (30:19-20).

Because God wanted to keep His people separate and pure, violation of the Law was often punishable by death. For example, if a man had intercourse with another man's wife, both were to be put to death. "In this way you will get rid of this evil," God explained (22:22).

Other laws were intended to protect the honor of women according to the standards of that day. For instance, if a man raped an engaged woman, he was to be killed. If he raped a woman who was not engaged, he was to take her as his wife and never divorce her as long as he lived (22:28-29).

The Law teaches us much about God. Above all, He expects and demands respect. The tassels on clothes were to remind the people of the Ten Commandments, in which we are told to have no other gods. The Lord also requires justice: "An eye for an eye; a tooth for a tooth" (19:21). He demonstrates compassion and concern; the railing around the flat-roofed houses was to keep people from falling off and hurting themselves.

And God encourages joy in worship! In establishing religious festivals, God said: "Be joyful because the Lord has blessed your harvest and your work. . . . Be joyful in the Lord's presence, together with your children, your servants, and the Levites, foreigners, orphans, and widows who live in your towns" (16:15, 11).

Over and over God provided for widows and orphans. "Do not deprive . . . orphans of their rights," He says, "and do not take a widow's garment for a loan." Some of the grain, olives, and grapes were to be left in the fields for widows to harvest. Moreover, when the

Law was read to the people every seven years, women and children were to be included too so they could learn (31:12).

Yes, thanks to God's Word in Deuteronomy and Christ's sacrifice on the cross, women also can "choose life" and be assured of blessings by following the Lord's will.

LET'S PRAY: Most Holy God, we marvel at Your greatness, Your power, Your miracles—and Your willingness to forgive us every time we repent of our sins. Thank You for encouraging fairness and justice for women as well as for men. Help us remain faithful to You and be joyful and thankful for Your blessings. In Jesus' name. Amen.

Prayer

Praying Is Believing

D escribng a woman of tremendous faith and prayer, someone said, "She's the type of Christian who, if asked to pray for rain, would carry an umbrella to her place of prayer."

Yes, God can and often does provide immediate answers to prayer, as the members of Mrs. Carl Walther's sewing circle discovered in the mid-1850s. During one of their meetings to mend the clothing of students at Concordia Seminary in St. Louis, the women were lamenting the extremely dry weather. As their complaints continued, Mrs. Walther said, "My dear friends, we don't pray enough; this drought is due partly to the lack of prayer. Let us all kneel and fervently petition the Lord to send us rain." The women did as she suggested, and before the end of their meeting, they heard "sounds of rolling thunder, the sun became obscured, clouds gathered, lightning flashed . . . and a welcome rain refreshed the parched earth."[1]

Prayer has been described as "a dialogue between two people who love each other—God and man/woman." More specifically, it is communication with God, communication that is to continue without ceasing.

Joshua is the perfect example of constant communication with the Lord. The successor to Moses, Joshua consulted the Lord before every decision in relation to the conquest of Canaan—and the Lord kept His promise to be with him wherever he went.

The invasion of the Promised Land was an exciting and remarkable time for the people of Israel. Led by the Lord, they emerged victorious in battle after battle.

The details are shared in the Book of Joshua. Among
its highlights are
- the escape of the spies from Jericho with the aid of
  Rahab, the prostitute, who helped them out her
  window and down the city wall with a rope;
- the crossing of the Jordan River, while its flood
  waters were halted by the Lord;
- the takeover of Jericho when the walls came tum-
  bling down, after the priests and soldiers had
  marched around the city blowing trumpets for
  seven days in a row;
- the defeat of the Amorites as the sun stood still in
  the middle of the sky and did not go down for a
  whole day;
- the establishment of cities of refuge for those who
  accidentally killed someone; and
- the assignment of territories to each of the 12
  tribes.

Thus it could truly be said, "The Lord kept every
one of the promises that he had made to the people of
Israel" (21:45).

With his work completed, Joshua died at age 110,
but not until all the people of Israel had vowed, "As for
my family and me, we will serve the Lord." They had
seen His answers to prayers—and so have we in the
Book of Joshua.

In those same pages, we also meet a woman who
demonstrates in her relationship with her father the
confidence we should have in our communication with
the Lord. The woman is Achsah, the daughter of Caleb.
When she was being married, her father gave Achsah
dry land as a dowry. Dry land in that hot climate was
not very productive. Therefore, she approached her father with a request for some waterholes. He responded
by giving her both upper and lower springs.

So too the Lord will generously answer our needs
when we remain faithful to Him and in communication
with Him. What a blessing that He not only allows but
also wants and invites us to pray . . . and likewise promises to answer!

LET'S PRAY: Lord, we thank You for providing a way for us to communicate with You and for promising to answer our prayers. Bless us and guide us so that we may always do Your will. In Jesus' name. Amen.

Leadership

When the Lord Taps You on the Shoulder

The 20th century has been filled with firsts for women seeking leadership opportunities in government. We can think of Geraldine Ferraro, first woman nominated for the vice-presidency of the United States by a major political party; Margaret Chase Smith, first woman elected to the U.S. Senate; Margaret Thatcher, first woman prime minister of England; Sandra Day O'Connor, first woman appointed to the Supreme Court; and Jane Byrne, first woman mayor of Chicago.

The list could go on. But few will ever equal the accomplishments of Deborah, an Old Testament judge and ruler over God's people. Deborah is one of three women identified as prophets in the Old Testament.

Her story is told in the Book of Judges. This book covers the period from the invasion of Canaan to the time when God provided kings to rule God's chosen people. Because they did not drive out all the pagans when they took over the Promised Land, the people of God frequently succumbed to the idol worship of those who lived in their midst. This angered the Lord, and He allowed their enemies to overpower them.

Whenever the Israelites repented, God sent a new leader to rescue them. "But when the leader died," according to Judges 2:19, "the people would return to the old ways and behave worse than the previous generation."

Judges records 12 such cycles of repentance rewarded by new leadership. The fourth of the God-given leaders was Deborah. In her day, the Israelites had been conquered by Jabin, a Canaanite king. Daily Deborah sat under a particular palm tree, listening to her people's problems and disputes and rendering wise decisions. Judges describes her as the "mother of Israel," a sign of the respect she merited.

One day she told Barak to gather 10,000 men to fight Jabin. She assured Barak that God would give him victory even though Jabin's army had 900 iron chariots. Barak refused to go into battle unless Deborah went with him. She agreed but informed him that, as a result, a woman—not he—would get credit for the victory.

As the battle got under way, the Lord sent rains, miring down some of the chariots and washing away others. The confused enemy forces were easily overcome. Sisera, the enemy commander, fled on foot. Seeking rest, he stopped at the tent of Jael, a Bedouin woman sympathetic to the Israelites. After giving him milk and cream, Jael waited until Sisera fell asleep and then drove a tent peg through his head, killing him. Thanks to her courage and strength, victory was assured for Israel.

The Bible describes Jael as "most fortunate of women." Does that seem strange to you? Obviously, the passage is not intended to encourage women to kill their enemies, but the stories of both Jael and Deborah do support women's courageous use of their God-given talents in the work of their Lord and their country. Deborah, for instance, was selected for her role at a time when men like Phinehas, the grandson of Aaron, were alive and available for the post. More importantly, the Lord blessed Deborah's rule with peace in the land for 40 years!

Despite God's blessing of women leaders in this and other Biblical instances, the leadership role is not one which most women find comfortable. At its 1985 convention, an international churchwomen's organization changed the name of its Christian Leadership Training Committee to Member Support Committee because so many members were hesitant to use leadership training materials and attend leadership training seminars.

Evidently little has changed since the group's organizational meeting in 1942. Many participants then hesitated about or refused nomination for office until a wise pastoral counselor advised: "When the Lord taps you on the shoulder and says, 'I need you for this job,' you must not turn Him down. If He did not think you could do it, He would not have chosen you."

At such a time, perhaps women need to remember another passage in Scripture, "With God, nothing is impossible"—and His great promise, "I am with you always." Because of this assurance and the example of Deborah, we women *can* say YES when the Lord taps us on the shoulder for a special assignment.

LET'S PRAY: Dear Lord, thank You for Your encouragement and support—and for the example of Deborah. Give us courage to walk through the doors You open to us. In Jesus' name. Amen.

Family of God

Your People Will Be My People

*H*ave you ever thought to yourself: "I don't see how God can possibly care about me. After all, nobody loves me. I have so few friends. I'm ugly. I'm too fat (or too thin); I'm too short (or too tall). My skin is the wrong color—or my nationality isn't well-liked."

Or perhaps you've said: "I don't think God even knows I exist. I'm so insignificant . . . so worthless. I always seem to do everything wrong. I'm such a sinner."

Some of those statements apply to four women of the Bible whom the Lord blessed despite their sins, their profession, or their nationality—and thereby He demonstrates the inclusiveness of the family of God. They are Tamar, an unwed mother; Bathsheba, an adulteress; Rahab, a prostitute; and Ruth, a Gentile. Let's meet them individually.

Tamar is the wife of Er, a grandson of Jacob, but Er is so evil that the Lord kills him. Then Judah, Er's father, tells his second son, Onan, to sleep with Tamar so that a child might be born in his brother's name. Because the child would belong to his brother, Onan lets his seed go on the ground, so the Lord kills him also. After Er's death, Judah tells Tamar to return to her family until his third son, Shelah, grows up. She obeys and remains in widow's clothes for years, waiting for Judah to keep his promise to make Shelah her husband. Then Judah's wife dies. Hearing that Judah is traveling to Timnath for sheepshearing, Tamar disguises herself as a prostitute. With her face veiled, she waits by the roadside, and Judah seeks her favors. She becomes pregnant and gives birth to twins, one of whom becomes an ancestor of Jesus.

Bathsheba's story is one of passion, intrigue, and

murder. When David sees the beautiful Bathsheba bathing on the roof of a nearby house, he sends for her, even though she is married, and she becomes pregnant as a result of their relationship. To hide his indiscretion, David places her husband, Uriah, in the front battle lines so that he will be killed. David then marries Bathsheba; their son, however, dies one week after birth. Later the Lord blesses the repentant couple with another son, Solomon, who also becomes an ancestor of Jesus.

Rahab, a prostitute in Jericho, lives in a house built into the city wall. When the Hebrews send two spies to Jericho, she hides them in her home and helps them escape. As a result, she and her family are saved when Jericho is destroyed. She later marries one of the spies and becomes the mother of Boaz and thus an ancestor of Jesus.

That brings us to the beautiful story of **Ruth,** a Gentile, that is, a foreigner or heathen. During a time of famine in Israel, Naomi and her husband move to Moab, a country occupied by descendants of Lot. Later Naomi's husband dies, as well as her two sons, who have married Moabites.

When Naomi decides to return to her homeland, one of her daughters-in-law, Ruth, urges Naomi, "Don't ask me to leave you! Let me go with you. Wherever you go, I will go; wherever you live, I will live. Your people will be my people, and your God will be my God." Naomi agrees.

In Israel, Ruth gleans grain in the fields to provide food for the two—and there she meets the wealthy Boaz. Attracted by Ruth's beauty and moved by her loyalty to her mother-in-law and her devotion to the Lord, Boaz arranges to marry Ruth. Their son Jesse becomes the grandfather of King David—and this means that Ruth, too, is a part of the lineage of Christ.

Told in just four chapters, the Book of Ruth is one of the most charming love stories in the Bible. But coupled with the stories of the other three women linked to the line of Christ, it reassures all of us of the forgiveness of the Lord and the inclusiveness of the family of God. We need only to repent and trust in the love of our Lord and Savior to be assured of acceptance here on earth and a home in heaven with all believers.

LET'S PRAY: Thank You, Lord, for the examples of forgiveness and blessing demonstrated in the lives of Ruth, Bathsheba, Rahab, and Tamar. Thank You also for bringing us into Your family of believers through the gift of faith in our Savior, Jesus Christ. Amen.

Wisdom

Common Sense Plus!

Complete this sequence: 1, 6, 3, 8, 5, 10, __, __ . Questions like this are often found in IQ tests and in examinations for persons who wish to join Mensa, an organization of people with high intelligence.

Supposedly questions of this type test the ability to think rather than the mere memorization of facts required to win TV game shows and Trivial Pursuit.

Even IQ tests, though, do not discover the existence of *wisdom,* which one dictionary defines as "common sense." But wisdom is more than that. It involves judgment and understanding, plus discrimination between good and evil. It relies on experience and requires vision and ability to plan.

Biblical wisdom is anchored in the Lord and applies His ways and His goals to our daily life.

When we mention the words "Biblical wisdom," we immediately think of Proverbs, with its many rules for happiness, and Ecclesiastes and Job, which explore the meaning of life and the relationship between God and His creation.

But for women seeking models of wisdom, no Biblical books surpass 1 and 2 Samuel. These two books cover the life of Samuel, the last and greatest of the judges, and Saul and David, the first two kings appointed by God. As we see Saul and David expand the Israelite territory in dozens of battles, it is obvious, as the *Good News Bible* explains in its introduction, that "faithfulness to God brings success, while disobedience brings disaster" (p. 294).

In three instances, disaster was prevented because of the quick thinking—the wisdom—of three women: Abigail, the wise woman of Abel, and the wife of the man in Bahurim. God's cause was also advanced because of two other wise women: Hannah and the wise woman of Tekoa.

Abigail was the wise wife of Nabal, whose name meant "fool." When Nabal refused to give David anything for protecting his flock of 4,000 sheep and goats, David became angry and set out to kill Nabal. Learning of the situation, Abigail gathered bread, wine, and other gifts without her husband's knowledge and presented them to David, telling him, "When the Lord . . . has made you king of Israel, then you will not have to feel regret or remorse . . . for having taken your own revenge" (1 Sam. 25:30-31). David thanked the Lord for Abigail's good sense, but Nabal had a stroke and died when he heard. David then married Abigail.

In those days, the Lord provided three classes of leaders for His people: the priests with the Law, the prophets with vision and the Word, and the wise with their counsel (Jer. 18:18; Ezek. 7:26).

Among the wise were the woman from Tekoa, who served as a mediator in reconciling David and his eldest son, Absalom, and the woman at Abel, who averted the destruction of her city by reasoning with David's soldiers as they besieged Abel. Learning that they were seeking Sheba, who had started a rebellion against David, the woman promised to throw Sheba's head over the wall to them. Then she persuaded the people of her city to kill Sheba, and the city was saved.

When Absalom attempted to take over David's throne, the woman in Bahurim saw two of David's spies hide in a cistern. She covered the cistern with a cloth and a pile of grain, thus protecting the spies from discovery. Her quick action enabled them to get word to David about the impending attack, and eventually David put down the rebellion.

Hannah set an example for all mothers in dedicating her son Samuel to the Lord and thus provided Israel with one of its most beloved leaders.

God blessed these women as they used their wisdom in their home, in their community, and in the cause of the Lord. And God, who is the same yesterday, today, and forever, will also supply us with wisdom and opportunity to use it to His glory if we but trust and obey Him.

LET'S PRAY: Lord, You have taught us that it is better to have wisdom and knowledge than gold and silver. Therefore, give us knowledge and understanding, but above all, give us wisdom that leads to salvation through faith in Christ Jesus. Amen.

Hospitality

The Bowl Did Not Run Out

During the depression of the 1930s, midwestern farmers claimed that the many hoboes who traversed the countryside had a way of marking the fences of the farms to let other hoboes know which families were hospitable and would provide a free meal.

Elijah and Elisha didn't need marked fences; they had the Lord directing them. Elijah's time of need arose when the Lord sent three years of drought to Israel in punishment for their sins. After Elijah announced the Lord's unpopular decision, he was told to hide near Cherith Brook. The brook would supply water, and the Lord would send ravens to bring food to him.

When the brook dried up because of lack of rain, the Lord sent Elijah to the home of a widow in Zarephath. She gave him water but informed him that she had no bread. All she had left was a handful of flour and a bit of olive oil. She intended to prepare this for herself and her son, she explained, adding, "That will be our last meal, and then we will starve to death" (1 Kings 17:12).

Elijah told her not to worry and asked her to make a small loaf for him first and then prepare the rest for herself and her son. He promised her that the bowl would not run out of flour or the jar run out of oil before the day that the Lord would send rain (1 Kings 17:14). And it was true!

In Elisha's case, he had gone to Shunem. There a rich woman "urged him to stay for a meal. So whenever he came by, he stopped there to eat. She said to her husband, 'I know that this man who often comes our way is a holy man of God. Let's make a small room on the roof and put in it a bed and a table, a chair and a lamp for him. Then he can stay there whenever he comes to us' " (2 Kings 4:8-10 NIV).

How many of us would do that today? Perhaps you're thinking: It would cost too much! Zoning laws wouldn't allow a room on the roof. It isn't safe; you can't trust strangers, even if they appear to be holy!

Unfortunately, failure to exercise Christian hospitality can cause us to miss out on blessings. As Hebrews 13:2 reminds us, "Remember to welcome strangers in your homes. There were some who did that and welcomed angels without knowing it."

In the Zarephath case, the blessing was the saved life of the widow's sick son. In the Shunem situation, Elisha sought a way to express his appreciation to his hostess. Realizing that she had no children, Elisha promised her a son, and the Lord provided that blessing the next year. Some years later when the boy died, the Lord brought him back to life in response to Elisha's prayer.

That leads us to the major lesson to be learned from the two books of Kings: faithfulness to the Lord leads to blessings; unfaithfulness brings punishment and disaster.

The strange thing is that the kings never seemed to learn that lesson. Even those who instituted reforms and led the Israelites back to the true God and away from idol worship often became lax in the latter years of their reign. The most repeated sentence in the two books is "He, like his predecessors, sinned against the Lord." Even Solomon with all his wisdom turned from God to worship the idols of his foreign wives in his last years.

Unfortunately, we often are no different from the 40-plus kings in 1 and 2 Kings. We rely more on money in the bank than on trust in the Lord. We let our neighbors set our standards, and we fail to meet the needs of the poor. Our children, our cars, our homes, and our jobs become our idols.

Thank the Lord, though, that we know the Savior. All we have to do is sincerely repent and rely on His righteousness to cover our sins. Let's rejoice in that blessing and then strive harder to follow the example of the woman at Shunem and the widow of Zarephath.

LET'S PRAY: Lord, we are so grateful for Your willingness to forgive and forgive and forgive in the name of Christ. Help us daily to be more appreciative of Your love, more understanding of the needs of others, and more willing to "practice hospitality ungrudgingly to one another" as You tell us in Your Word. We pray in Jesus' name. Amen.

Building

The Lord Knows!

The statement is so simple, so unassuming. You almost miss it if you aren't watching for it. It's just one verse: "Ephraim had a daughter named Sheerah. She built the towns of Upper and Lower Beth Horon, and Uzzen Sheerah" (7:24).

A woman building three towns in Old Testament times? It's a good thing the Bible identifies her sex because when you mention her accomplishments to some people, their first question is, "How do you know Sheerah was a woman?"

Yet there she is in the First Book of Chronicles.

Written just after the Jews returned from their Babylonian exile, the two Chronicles trace the whole of sacred history from Adam to Zerubbabel—more than 3,500 years in 70 pages! In contrast with the more political approach of 1 and 2 Samuel and 1 and 2 Kings, the two books of Chronicles offer religious history with a purpose.

The first nine chapters are family trees and lists of the tribes, priests, musicians, and temple guards of the Southern Kingdom. The tendency is to scan these chapters, but if we skim too rapidly, we miss some unusual sidelights . . . like Sheerah and her construction projects.

Chronicles next reports how David and Solomon preserved true worship and how David planned and Solomon built the temple. Finally, the author, who some think may have been Ezra, reviews the religious practices of the Southern kings and their followers. Once again, the message is that faithfulness to God and His commands brings peace and prosperity, while disobedience and worship of false gods results in problems and disaster. By recounting how the Lord kept His promises throughout the history of His chosen people, the intent of the books is to inspire total devotion to the Lord and full dedication to rebuilding the temple.

Building in those days was not simple. The construction of the original temple is a prime example. Solomon used 70,000 people to transport materials and 80,000 to cut stones in the mountains. This required 3,600 supervisors to make sure the work was done (2 Chron. 2:18).

What a shame that Solomon's temple was destroyed, for it must have been uniquely beautiful! Tons of gold, silver, bronze, and iron were used, plus precious stones of all kinds. Cedar, cypress, and juniper logs were brought from Lebanon. The entire interior was paneled with wood and overlaid with fine gold, decorated in chain patterns and palm tree designs. Even the nails were of gold—and so were the pans for carrying live coals!

The homes in the towns that Sheerah constructed were undoubtedly much simpler. Those of wealthier people were normally made of stone, brick, and timber—and sometimes marble and ivory. Houses of the poor, however, were often one-room hovels with mud or clay walls. Reinforced with reeds and rushes, they sometimes became breeding places for rodents and snakes, for Amos speaks of "a man who comes home and puts his hand on the wall—only to be bitten by a snake!" (Amos 5:19).

We know almost nothing about Sheerah today. The cities she built never became large or famous. They exist nowadays under other names, but it doesn't matter. The Lord knows what she did, just as He knows all that we do. Whatever our talents, whether they include building cities or baking bread, they are to be used to His glory and for the good of His people.

That's what Sheerah did, and that's what we must do.

LET'S PRAY: Dear Lord, we stand in awe of Your power and majesty. You have done marvelous things for Your people of the Old Testament—and for us today. Help us tell everyone what You have done, and continue to keep us in Your protection. In Jesus' name. Amen.

Prophecy

In the Footsteps of Huldah

What does a prophet do? Most people would probably respond: "Prophets foretell the future." That idea intrigues us, because we are all by nature curious. We'd like to know what's going to happen tomorrow and next week and next year.

People make millions today trying to do just that. Thousands of business publications attempt to predict what the stock market will do. Advertising researchers seek to discover whether a new product will sell. Millions watch weather forecasts nightly to learn if it will be rainy or sunny the next day.

Although Biblical prophets sometimes did foretell the future, their basic role was of far greater importance. They were to be spokespersons for God. The Hebrew word for prophet means "one who is inspired by God."

God often sent Old Testament prophets on daring missions with messages that were most unpopular, as we shall see later in the books of the prophets. The goal was to call God's people to repentance by showing them their sins. As a result, the prophets were sometimes afraid and ran away like Jonah. Others were undaunted but found themselves imprisoned or, like Daniel, were thrown into the lions' den.

In 2 Chronicles, though, it was not the prophet who went to the people but the people who sought the prophet . . . or rather the prophetess.

It happened during the reign of King Josiah. He became king at the age of only 8 years, and when he was 16, he began to worship the God of King David, his ancestor. The result was reform! He smashed the altars to false gods and goddesses and tore down the idols. He killed the pagan priests and burned their bones in the places where they had worshiped.

After making Judah ritually clean again, he placed three men in charge of repairing the temple. There in a storeroom, they discovered the Book of the Law. When a portion was read to the king, who was now 26 years old, he tore his clothes in dismay and immediately ordered the priest to "go and consult the Lord for me and for the people who still remain in Israel and in Judah. Find out about the teachings of this book" (34:21).

The priest went not to the male prophets, but to Huldah, a prophetess who lived in the newer part of Jerusalem. She conveyed this message from the Lord: "I am going to bring disaster on this place and its people—all the curses written in the book that has been read in the presence of the king of Judah. . . . my anger will be poured out on this place and will not be quenched" (34:24-25 NIV). Since the king had repented and already instituted reforms, Huldah assured him that the Lord had heard his prayer and the punishment would not occur until after his death.

Deeply distressed, nevertheless, Josiah gathered all the people of Judah together, read the whole book to them, and made them all promise to keep the covenant. Then he began a purge of all the territory belonging to the people of Israel. He tore down altars dedicated to demons, to Asherah (the pagan "Queen" of the Heavens), to Baal and Milcom, and to the sun, moon, planets, and stars. He also removed all the mediums and fortunetellers, all the household gods, idols, and other pagan objects of worship.

Then they celebrated the Passover—for seven whole days! Not since the days of Samuel had the Passover been celebrated like that!

How we women could rejoice too if only all prophetesses had the integrity of Huldah. Later in Ezekiel we find the Lord denouncing women who make up predictions: "You women are doomed!" He says. "You sew magic wristbands for everyone and make magic scarves for everybody to wear on their heads, so that they can have power over other people's lives. You want to possess the power of life and death over my people and to use it for your own benefit.... By your lies you discourage good people, whom I do not wish to hurt" (Ezek. 13:18, 22).

These women killed people and lied to them. What a contrast to Huldah! What an example for us! Today as women teach and evangelize, may our goal be to follow in the footsteps of Huldah, and may the message we proclaim be inspired by the gift of the Holy Spirit, which our Lord in the Book of Joel promised to pour out on everyone, including women and daughters (2:28-29).

LET'S PRAY: Lord, we want to be faithful; we want to be like Huldah, a blessing to Your people. Pour out Your Holy Spirit on each of us so that we may share Your message wherever and whenever You would have us do so. In Jesus' name. Amen.

Family Unity

Opposites Attract!

A nyone seeking proof that opposites attract should read the Bible! Over and over we find Old Testament men marrying "foreign" wives, pagans who had been living in the Promised Land which God gave to the Israelites. In each case God objected, not because these women were of another culture or tribe, but because they worshiped false gods and led their husbands and their children to abandon the true God.

God's goal, as stated repeatedly in the Old Testament, was to set His people apart as a holy nation . . . to make them separate and distinct . . . a people consecrated to His holy purposes.

Even though God's appointed leaders repeatedly reminded the people of the blessings which the Lord had showered on them during the years of the Exodus, still the people turned time after time to the pagans in the lands where they settled . . . turned to them not only as friends but also as spouses.

This always led to the worship of Baal and the practices of the fertility cults. Even Gideon, after God gave him victory in Midian, gathered the earrings the people had taken from the Midianites and "made an idol from the gold and put it in his hometown" and "all the Israelites abandoned God and went there to worship the idol" (Judges 8:27).

When Ahab, the seventh king of the Northern Kingdom of Israel, married Jezebel, a Baal worshiper, he built a temple to Baal at his capital in Samaria and also put up an image of the goddess Asherah. The priests, of course, objected, but Jezebel silenced their objections by having them killed. In punishment, God sent a three-year drought.

To a great degree, though, the Israelites did learn the lesson of faithfulness to God during the Babylonian captivity. Their return to Jerusalem is described in the Book of Ezra. They returned in three stages:

• The first group came in 538/7 B.C. with the approval of the Persian emperor, who said, "You are to go to Jerusalem and rebuild the temple of the Lord," and he provided the supplies to do it. This group fulfilled their assignment and dedicated the new temple.

• The second group, 80 years later, was led by Ezra, an expert in God's law and the priest whom Jewish tradition credits with arranging the canon of the Old Testament. ("Canon" comes from a Greek word meaning a reed or rod used as a measuring stick; so canon means the official list of authoritative writings.)

• The third wave came with Nehemiah in 445 B.C.

When Ezra returned from the Captivity, he discovered that despite the accomplishments of the first group, opposites had once again attracted, and a number of Jewish men had married foreign wives. In the words of Ezra, "they were doing the same disgusting things" which the heathens did. Crushed with grief, Ezra tore his hair, his beard, and his clothes. Then bowing in prayer in front of the temple, he confessed their sins. Men, women, and children gathered around him and began weeping bitterly.

Finally a man named Shecaniah said, "We have broken faith with God by marrying foreign women, but even so there is still hope for Israel. Now we must make a solemn promise to our God that we will send these women and their children away" (10:2-3).

And that's just what they did. They divorced the foreign wives and sent them and their children away (10:44). Does that sound harsh? Perhaps—but let's remember what it also says about the persuasive powers of a woman in her role as wife and mother. There is truth to the adage: The hand that rocks the cradle rules the world.

How important the faith of the wife is as a role model in marriage—and it is no less important today than it was in Old Testament times, for 2 Corinthians 6:14-15 tells us: "Do not try to work together as equals with unbelievers, for it cannot be done. How can right and wrong be partners? How can light and darkness live together? How can Christ and the Devil agree? What does a believer have in common with an unbeliever?"

The answer is nothing! A strong and happy marriage requires unity, not only in personal goals but also in faith.Ezra understood that, and it's still true today.

LET'S PRAY: Lord, grant us strong Christian marriages and unity of faith in our families so that Your Word may be shared and honored by succeeding generations. In Jesus' name. Amen.

Perseverance

Tough on the Outside—
Sweet on the Inside

our guides in the Holy Land often claim the cactus is the flower of Israel. The cactus, they say, is like the Jewish people—tough on the outside but sweet on the inside.

Nowhere is that toughness and perseverance more evident than in the history of Jerusalem. The focal point in the development of three world religions—Judaism, Christianity, and Islam—this city has been destroyed and rebuilt 10 times in the last 3,000 years.

Still it exists and grows, despite modern-day disputes between the Christians and Jews who live there. Today all Israeli men are trained as soldiers, and some of the teenage young men regularly carry military rifles on the streets. Here and there tanks and cannons from more recent wars stand as grim reminders that destruction could occur all over again, just as it did at the time of the Babylonian captivity of the Israelites. (Then thousands died, some fled to the wilderness, and others succumbed to disease and starvation as the city was left in ashes, and an estimated 18,000 leaders and their families were deported to Babylon.)

About 50 years later these people received permission to return and rebuild the temple, and a number of them did just that. However, after 90 years in Jerusalem, much also remained undone. When Nehemiah learned that the walls were still broken down and "the gates had not been restored since the time they were burned," he sat down and wept in Babylon (1:3-4). For four months this devout man of God mourned, and then he decided it was time for action. Not only was his request for permission to return to Jerusalem granted, but he was appointed governor of the province.

Upon arrival in Jerusalem, he surveyed the situation and then told the people: "See what trouble we are in because Jerusalem is in ruins and its gates are destroyed! Let's rebuild the city walls and put an end to our disgrace" (2:17).

"Let's start rebuilding!" the people agreed, and each family took responsibility for a section of the wall. In the section assigned to Shallum, the ruler of half of Jerusalem, his daughters helped with the work (3:12). It wasn't easy work, and it wasn't "women's work" in that day, but they undoubtedly did it because it was important to the security of their home, and it was what the Lord wanted.

The perseverance of all the workers paid off! Even though it took 28 months to finish the gates and battlements, the wall itself was secure in just 52 days!

How often women today are also called to rebuild. Sometimes it may be physical rebuilding that's needed, like a home destroyed by fire or flood or tornado. More often though, it is the rebuilding of a relationship or a life: a marriage broken by separation or divorce, a relative addicted to drugs or drinking, a family fighting poverty after loss of a job, a child frightened by abuse, refugees adjusting to a new homeland, or an elderly neighbor haunted by fear of robbery or dread of death.

Christian women can be an influence for good in all these situations, but perhaps our greatest challenge, like that facing Christian men, is to persevere in faith and share that faith with everyone whose life touches ours. To encourage us to persevere, the New Testament offers some good advice: "Be persistent in prayer" (Col. 4:2). "You must not become tired of doing good" (2 Thess. 3:13). And finally: "Keep up your eagerness to the end so that the things you hope for will come true" (Heb. 6:11).

LET'S PRAY: Dear Lord, we are eager to do Your work and share Your Good News. Give us the strength to persevere in whatever rebuilding projects You set before us. In Jesus' name. Amen.

Principles

If I Must Die . . .

P lanning a gathering or a celebration of any kind is a big project, but when your guests are spread from India to Ethiopia and include people in 127 provinces . . . well, a party of that magnitude staggers the imagination.

Yet that's just what King Xerxes of Persia did during the Babylonian captivity of the Jewish people. He invited his officials, administrators, army officers, governors, and noblemen to his winter palace in Susa to show off the riches of his court, and he invited them not for a day or a week, but for six months!

Then when that ended, he invited all the people of Susa, rich and poor alike, to the palace for a dinner that lasted seven days! That's the setting for the Book of Esther.

Wine flowed in abundance as the king entertained the men in the courtyard of the palace garden. It was elegantly decorated with marble pillars, beautiful tapestries, gold and silver couches, and floors of alabaster, marble, turquoise, and mother-of-pearl. Since women and men never intermingled at such events, Queen Vashti gave a banquet inside the palace for the women.

On the seventh day when the king was feeling happy after all that drinking, he decided to show off the beauty of the queen to his drunken guests. A woman of principle, the modest queen refused, and in his anger the king divorced her! Wouldn't it be great if women in this age of the centerfold magazine had her strength of character?

Four years later the king chose Esther, a Jewish virgin, as his new queen. The new consort was a woman of God, a woman chosen by God "for such a time as this," a woman chosen to save her people.

Not knowing that Esther was Jewish, King Xerxes was coerced into signing a decree that all the Jewish people living in his kingdom should be killed. Young and old, women and children—all "were to be slaughtered without mercy and their belongings were to be taken" for the royal treasury (3:13).

You must plead with the king to have mercy on your people, Esther was told—but it wasn't that simple. By law, anyone who went to the inner courtyard to see the king without being summoned would be put to death. Esther had not been summoned for a month. Her only hope was that the king might hold out his scepter to her as she approached him, for then her life would be spared.

Courageously she agreed, saying, "If I must die for doing it, I will die" (4:16).

Asking all the Jews in Susa to fast and pray for three days, and after doing the same herself, Esther then approached her husband. He held out his scepter! In fact, he went even further: "What is it, Queen Esther?" the king asked. "Tell me what you want and you shall have it—even if it is half my empire" (5:3).

Without Esther's intervention, there would have been no Nehemiah, no Mary and Joseph, no Jesus. Today the Jewish people still celebrate the Feast of Purim in thanksgiving for their rescue, and at the annual commemoration of the event, they always read the Book of Esther.

The story of Esther is proof that God cares for His own through ordinary people like you and me, through people like a Jewish orphan named Esther. The early church father Tertullian has said that "Christians are to society what the soul is to the body." This is true only when Christians are willing to stand up and be counted, willing to risk their security for what they know is right, willing to follow in the footsteps of women like Vashti and Esther.

LET'S PRAY: Dear Lord, give us the courage of

Esther and Vashti to stand up today for what we know is right. Let the influence of true Christianity be felt in this country—and let it begin with me. In Jesus' name. Amen.

Problems/ Blessings

Twice Blest!

Let's play a word association game. Mention the first Biblical person who comes to mind when you hear the words "problems" or "suffering." One of the most likely answers is Job, the wealthy patriarch from the land of Uz who lost everything.

Now mention the first Biblical person who comes to mind when you hear the words "twice blest" or "highly blest." Probably dozens of names enter our thoughts—and none of them are Job. But could Job be the answer?

The Book of Job is the first of three books, including Proverbs and Ecclesiastes, which are identified as "wisdom literature." It is also the first of five poetical books in the Old Testament. It is the book that asks the unanswerable question, "If God is just and good, why does He allow innocent people to suffer?"

Job was a genuinely good man—as good as any human being can possibly be. He treated his servants fairly; he helped the poor; he was faithful to his wife; he never trusted in riches nor worshiped false gods.

Satan tells God that Job is so good only because of the benefits he receives—the blessings the Lord has showered on him. He owns thousands of sheep, camels, cattle, and donkeys. He has many servants and 10 fine children. He is the richest man in the East.

Satan asks the Lord, "Would Job worship You if he got nothing out of it?" The Lord agrees to a test. The only thing Satan may not do is take Job's life.

When Job loses his possessions, his servants, and

his children, he remains loyal to the Lord. Then Satan says Job's only real concern is himself, so the Lord agrees to a further test. Satan afflicts Job's body with boils. At this point, his wife fails him, and three friends who come to comfort him actually indulge in verbal torture as they accuse him of great sins.

As the dialog continues, Job reveals that selfish motives do exist in him. "I hoped for happiness and light," he admits (30:26). Finally, as all of us must do, he throws himself on the mercy of the Lord. "I am ashamed of all I have said and repent in dust and ashes," he concludes.

Then once again—for the second time in Job's life—the Lord showers him with blessings. He becomes wealthier than before. He has another 10 children, including 3 daughters. Although the Bible does not name the sons, it identifies each of the daughters. Their names suggest beauty both in sound and in meaning. The oldest is Jemimah, or "dove." The second is Keziah, or "cassia," which is a variety of cinnamon used as perfume. The third, Keren Happuch, is the name of a small box used for eye make-up (*Good News Bible,* p. 593). The Bible says, "There were no other women in the whole world as beautiful as Job's daughters. Their father gave them a share of the inheritance along with their brothers" (42:15).Women can learn at least three lessons from Job:

1. We can rejoice that his daughters were considered among his greatest blessings and were treated equally with his sons.

2. We can see the importance of wives remaining steadfast in their faith and thereby supporting their husbands in time of trial. Although Scripture has many examples of women who are strong, it introduces us to just as many who are like Job's wife. How sad to hear her say, "Why don't you curse God and die?"

3. God's ultimate answer to Job is a question: "Who are you to question my wisdom?" God reminds Job that it is He, the Lord, who created the earth, commands day to dawn, and sends the rain and the sun. In response, Job acknowledges that God is all powerful. We too must understand this and entrust ourselves unquestionably to this almighty Lord of the universe, who assures us, just as He did Job, that He does love us and care for us. That's all we need to know!

LET'S PRAY: Almighty and all-powerful Lord, we thank You for creating us and caring for us. Even though we don't always understand Your ways, we trust You, and we know that because of Your love, our blessings will always outnumber our sorrows. We pray gratefully, in Jesus' name. Amen.

Sing

Make a Joyful Noise Unto the Lord!

As millions of refugees from Chinese Communism streamed into Hong Kong in the 50s, they had nothing . . . no clothing, food, money, or home. But they found something worth far more; they found Christ.

Many met the Savior through Gertrude Simon, a Lutheran missionary who would walk into their midst singing and then urge them to join her. Her song was always the same: "How Sweet the Name of Jesus Sounds" and her invitation was always the same: "Sing with me . . . Sing with me!"

They sang. And through the singing, they learned about the Lord, and they gave thanks to Him, just as people have done since the days of the psalmists.

From those earliest times, music—or joyful noise, as the Bible sometimes calls it—has been an important part of worship and religious ritual. King David's Egyptian wife brought a dowry of 1,000 musical instruments with her, and David invented still others. First Chronicles 23:5 describes how he appointed 4,000 men "to praise the Lord with the musical instruments . . . provided for that purpose" (NIV). Next he named 280 singers to serve as chief musicians to teach the 4,000 and to lead the worship services, accompanied by harps and cymbals.

When Solomon's temple was dedicated, 120 priests sounded the trumpets, and all the singers united as one voice to sing and praise the Lord. What a thrill that must have been! It was at that moment that the temple "was suddenly filled with a cloud shining with the dazzling light of the Lord's presence" (2 Chron. 5:14).

One hundred and fifty of the Hebrew hymns and litanies have been retained for us in Psalms, the hymn-book of the Bible. Some of the psalms were sung by the Jewish people on pilgrimages to Jerusalem for religious festivals. In other words, they were the ballads of the people in the same way that Negro spirituals and Appalachian folk songs expressed the faith and prayers of those cultures.

Today, psalms are once again being set to modern melodies in youth hymnbooks. This is not new in the church. Many carols, for instance, were medieval dance tunes. Even Luther sang some of his doctrinal verses to secular melodies of his time. "Why should the devil have all the good tunes?" he asked.

Speaking of Luther, it's interesting that his famous hymn, "A Mighty Fortress Is Our God," was inspired by Psalm 46, which was written for "Alamoth"—that is, for soprano voices. Yes, women were involved in praising the Lord with song in those days too. In Psalm 68, a national song of triumph by David, the procession into the temple includes maidens playing tambourines, and Psalm 148 urges young women to praise Him too.

More recently, in keeping with the psalmist's directive to "sing a new song unto the Lord," women have also written hymns. Fanny Crosby, a 19th-century blind poet, composed 10,000 hymns and poems, 2,000 of which were published. Her most famous, "Blessed Assurance," was a favorite even in secular circles during the Gay Nineties. Ann Warner wrote the ever popular "Jesus Loves Me," and modern hymnals still include "O Savior, Precious Savior," "I Am Trusting You, Lord Jesus," and "Take My Life and Let It Be," all by Frances Havergal.

But music in our modern churches has a long way to go to match the fervor of Old Testament times. Psalm 150:3-5 urges: "Praise Him with trumpets. Praise Him with harps and lyres. Praise Him with drums and dancing. Praise Him with harps and flutes. . . . Praise Him with loud cymbals." Psalm 149:6 says, "Let them shout aloud as they praise God." Small wonder the Bible calls it a "joyful noise."

May our music likewise be enthusiastic, our creativeness evident, and our applause offerings echo from the rafters as we too "praise the Lord for His supreme greatness."

LET'S PRAY: Dear Lord, we praise You in our church and in our homes. We praise You for Your strength in heaven and for the mighty things You have done in our lives. We praise You for Your supreme greatness and for the love You have shown in sending Your Son as our Savior. Hallelujah! In Jesus' name. Amen. (Loud applause!)

Priorities

She Speaks with Gentle Wisdom

Tired of city living, a naïve young Chicago couple moved to Texas to try their hand at farming. After leasing a small piece of land, they decided they needed a mule to pull their plow.

At the first place they stopped, the owner said he had no mule for sale, but pointing to a pile of huge watermelons, he said he did have some mule eggs. "We'll hatch our own," the couple agreed and bought one. On the way home, their pickup truck hit a bump in the road, and the "egg" flew out the back, breaking open as it hit the pavement.

After they realized what had happened, the two turned around and drove back. Meanwhile a large, long-eared Texas jackrabbit had discovered the melon and begun to nibble. Frightened by the approaching truck, the rabbit took off across the field like a jet. Looking sadly at their disappearing "newborn mule," the woman said to the man, "Oh, well, I don't think you want to plow that fast anyway!"

Do you have the same reaction as you think about the ideal wife described in Proverbs 31? Do you feel tired just reading about her?

Not only does she spin her own thread, but she also weaves her own wool and linen cloth, making clothing and bed coverings for her family. Moreover, she's a businesswoman as well as a homemaker, for she makes clothing and belts to sell at a profit. She uses the money she earns to buy land and plant a vineyard.

Like a merchant ship, she brings food from faraway places, then gets up before daylight to prepare breakfast for her family and direct her servant girls.

She plans ahead too, for she makes sure there is

enough oil in her lamps to burn all night (For safety, the Israelites burned their lamps all night so that robbers would know their houses or tents were not deserted.)

This ideal woman is also "strong and respected and not afraid of the future" (31:25). She is always busy, never idle; always does good and never harm to her husband. Her children show their appreciation, and her husband, who is one of the community's leading citizens, praises her. He says, "Many women are good wives, but you are the best of them all" (31:29).

Her concern extends outside her home, too, for she is generous to the poor. More importantly, she reveres the Lord, and *she speaks with gentle wisdom.* Wouldn't it be great if everyone who knows us could say that about each of us?

But the question remains: How does she do it? Where does she get the time? Finding time—that's the problem for us today, too.

If any book in the Bible is to provide an answer, it should be Proverbs; for Proverbs is a collection of many of the 3,000 wise sayings of King Solomon. A book of practical ethics, it's the advice column of the Bible. It's full of helpful hints about marriage, friends, health ["Kind words are like honey . . . good for your health" (16:24)], old age, justice, charity—and priorities.

There we learn that our first priority should be wisdom, or understanding: "Get wisdom and insight! . . . Do not abandon wisdom, and she will protect you; love her, and she will keep you safe. . . . she will make you great. Embrace her, and she will bring you honor. She will be your crowning glory" (4:5-9).

Wisdom, though personified as a woman, is a foreshadowing of the Son of God. Unlike knowledge, which is simply an amassing of facts, wisdom is based on awe and respect for the Lord and obedience to His laws. When we seek first the kingdom of God, then all other goals and priorities fall into place, and He gives us the strength and shows us the way to accomplish more than we ever dreamed possible—even more, perhaps, than the ideal woman of Proverbs!

LET'S PRAY: Dear Lord, give us wisdom and insight, for we know from Proverbs that the wisdom You offer is more valuable than jewels; it makes our life on earth pleasant and leads us safely through this world to life eternal. This we ask in Jesus' name. Amen.

True Love

No Wonder All Women Love You!

D o you ever feel so discouraged that life seems futile? "What's the use?" we may ask. Or, as one man in the Bible put it, "You spend your life working, laboring and what do you have to show for it?" (Eccl. 1:3).

Take heart! The Lord understands, and the proof is in Ecclesiastes. There Solomon, the king who had everything—wisdom, wives galore, and all the accomplishments and treasure a person could desire—realizes that none of this means a thing. "It was like chasing the wind—of no use at all," he concludes (Eccl. 2:11).

Yet life is more than discouragement and despair, he acknowledges, if one reveres God and keeps His commandments. In fact, life is to be enjoyed, Solomon says, because it is a gift of God: "Go ahead—eat your food and be happy; drink your wine and be cheerful. It's all right with God. Always look happy and cheerful" (Eccl. 9:7-8).

Then he advises, "Enjoy life with the woman you love" (Eccl. 9:9). That statement provides the transition to the next book of the Bible, the Song of Solomon, a piece of literature in total contrast to Ecclesiastes. Seldom are two writings by the same author so opposite in tone. Someone has suggested that the Song of Solomon was written in Solomon's youth, Proverbs in middle age, and Ecclesiastes in old age.

A series of lyric poems, the Song of Solomon describes the beauty of true love between a man and a woman. As one author says, " . . . the poems as they stand celebrate the beauty and wonder of human love. There is a frank and open delight in physical attraction, which underlines the fact that God intends man to enjoy physical love within the laws he has given."[1]

And what woman—or what man—would not enjoy being told, in the words of Solomon, "Your love delights me. . . . Your love is better than wine; your perfume more fragrant than any spice. . . . The taste of honey is on your lips, my darling. . . . Your lips are like a scarlet ribbon; how lovely they are when you speak" (4:10-11 and 3).

What makes such words so truly special, though, is knowing that the Lord approves, for it is His approval that adds bliss to the marriage relationship and raises the love expressed therein to an almost spiritual realm of oneness and mutuality.

Sexual love as sanctioned by the Lord in marriage is never dirty or degrading. It never involves brutality, pornography, or a demand to "prove you love me." Rather such love is completely and freely given and enjoyed, just as our Lord loved the Israelites and Christ loves us.

And that brings us to the reason for the inclusion of Ecclesiastes and the Song of Solomon in the Bible. Both have been the subject of much debate. Because of its frankness and intimacy, there was a time in history when no Jew under 30 was allowed to read the Song of Solomon. It was accepted as sacred Scripture because the Jews understood it as an allegory of God's love for them, and we Christians interpret it as a portrayal of Christ's love for us. Likewise, Ecclesiastes is not a creed of despair but rather a demonstration that God never intended us to find final or total satisfaction in life, but rather in Him.

Since it is true, as Ecclesiastes says, that "there is nothing new under the sun" (1:9 NIV), then we can rejoice in knowing that our God, who is a God of order, has everything under control. "Everything that happens in this world happens at the time God chooses. . . . the time for birth and the time for death. . . . the time for sorrow and the time for joy" (Eccl. 3:1-4).

True joy comes in knowing that our marvelous

triune God truly loves us and that Christ loved us enough to give His life for us. To each of us He says, in the words of the Song of Solomon, you are "like a lily among thorns" (2:2), and to Him we respond, "No wonder all women love you!" (1:4).

LET'S PRAY: Thank You, Lord, for assuring us that there is a time to heal, a time to build, a time to laugh, a time to dance and a time for peace. Thank You for each day that gives us time to love You and to serve You. In Jesus' name. Amen.

Compassion

My Love for You Will Never End

A cartoon shows two people standing opposite a church, watching the congregation emerge after the Sunday service. Suddenly they can't believe their eyes! The members are joyously carrying their pastor out on their shoulders like a sports hero. In amazement, one observer says to the other: "I wonder what he preached on!"

It's a pity our parishes don't often get that excited about the Lord's Word. Surely, one of the most moving books of the Old Testament, one which should excite all of us, is Isaiah. Though not the last book of the Old Testament, it makes a great transition from the Old to the New Testament. No other prophet so beautifully balances God's passion for justice with His great compassion for people.

Isaiah has been called the "prince of the prophets." He lived in Jerusalem in the eighth century B.C. and prophesied for over 40 years. In response to the Lord's call, an actual vision of God Almighty, Isaiah responded immediately, despite fears of personal inadequacy, "I will go! Send me!"

Let's let Isaiah's words minister to us now as women:

- "The Lord is compassionate, and when you cry to Him for help, He will answer you. The Lord will make you go through hard times, but He Himself will be there to teach you, and you will not have to search for Him" (30:19-20).
- "The Lord is waiting to be merciful to you. He is ready to take pity on you because He always does what is right. Happy are those who put their trust in the Lord" (30:18).

- "Do not be afraid—I will save you. I have called you by name—you are Mine. When you pass through deep waters, I will be with you; your troubles will not overwhelm you. . . . you are precious to Me and . . . I love you and give you honor. Do not be afraid—I am with you!" (43:1-5).
- "My love for you will never end" (54:10).
- "How great the Lord is! He rules over everything. . . . He always protects His people and gives them wisdom and knowledge. Their greatest treasure is their reverence for the Lord" (33:5-6).
- "He will settle disputes among great nations. They will hammer their swords into plows and their spears into pruning knives" (2:4).

In a magnificent description of our heavenly home, Isaiah writes:

- "The blind will be able to see and the deaf will hear. The lame will leap and dance, and those who cannot speak will shout for joy. . . . They will reach Jerusalem with gladness, singing and shouting for joy. They will be happy forever, forever free from sorrow and grief"(35:5-6, 10).

To lonely widows, Isaiah says, "Your Creator will be like a husband to you" (54:5).

Yes, ours is a Lord who cares about widows and orphans, the sick and lame, the downtrodden and the poor, but such compassion has only temporal value.

The jewel of Isaiah, therefore, is in chapter 7, verse 14—the clearest and most direct prediction of the birth of our Savior in the Old Testament. There we learn: "The Lord himself will give you a sign: The virgin will be with child and will give birth to a son and will call him Immanuel" (NIV).

What great news! A Savior! Immanuel—God with us! Born of a woman—born to save all who believe. Born for *you,*born for *me.* Hallelujah!

LET'S PRAY: You care, Lord; You really care! What can we say but *thank You!* Thank You for Your compassion. Thank You for Your love and for our life . . . eternally. In Jesus' name. Amen.

Judgment

No "Put-Downs"

*I*t's easy for modern women to feel frustrated and hurt as they read the Old Testament prophets; so many sins and problems are described, explained, or reported by using allusions to women. For example, in speaking to Israel through Jeremiah, the Lord says:

- "You certainly know how to chase after lovers. Even the worst of women can learn from you" (2:33).
- "But like an unfaithful wife, you have not been faithful to Me" (3:20).
- "Look up at the hilltops. Is there any place where you have not acted like a prostitute? You waited for lovers along the roadside. . . . You have defiled the land with your prostitution" (3:2-3).
- "Have you seen what Israel, that unfaithful woman, has done? She has turned away from Me, and on every high hill and under every green tree she has acted like a prostitute" (3:6). The passage goes on to identify Judah as "Israel's unfaithful sister," who became a prostitute too and "was not at all ashamed. She defiled the land, and she committed adultery by worshipping stones and trees" (3:9).

    In Zechariah 5, there is a vision of a woman in a basket—and she represents wickedness.

    And in Ezekiel, the Lord continues:

- " 'Like mother, like daughter.' You really are your mother's daughter. She detested her husband and her children. You are like your sisters, who hated their husbands and their children" (16:44-45).

    The climax comes in Ezekiel 23 where the Lord pronounces judgment on the two sinful sisters, Oholah and Oholibah, who represent Samaria and Jerusalem.

He says, "Bring a mob to terrorize them and rob them. Let the mob stone them and attack them with swords, kill their children, and burn down their houses. Throughout the land I will put a stop to immorality, as a warning to every woman not to commit adultery as they did. And you two sisters—I will punish you for your immorality and your sin of worshipping idols. Then you will know that I am the Sovereign Lord" (23:46-48).

God, of course, exercised His sovereignty through the fall of Samaria to the Assyrians in 722/721 B.C. and over 100 years later through the fall of Jerusalem to the Babylonians. As He explains, "By my great power and strength I created the world, mankind and all the animals that live on the earth; and I give it to anyone I choose" (Jer. 27:5). His requirement for believers (Is. 28:17) is faith that is firm and patient, faith built on a foundation of justice and honesty—and that applies to both men and women.

But getting back to all those feminine allusions:

1. We women must remember that we *are* sinners. We often fail to be faithful to the Lord. When the condemnation fits, we must repent. Then we too will hear those encouraging words which the Lord spoke in response to the allegorical weeping of Rachel: "There is hope for your future" (Jer. 31:16).

2. We must realize that our Lord does not indulge in "put-downs" of women. Often, in fact, He uses feminine comparisons to explain His own feelings and actions. In Isaiah 42:14 He says, "I cry out like a woman in labor." In Isaiah 49:15, when the people of Jerusalem think He has abandoned them, the Lord gives this comforting answer, "Can a woman forget her own baby and not love the child she bore? Even if a mother should forget her child, I will never forget you." And in Hosea 11, He describes His almost maternal love for His people, "I was the one who taught Israel to walk. . . . I drew [my people] to Me with affection and love. I picked them up and held them to my cheek; I bent down to them and fed them" (11:3-4).

3. We must remember the purpose of prophecy—to bring about change, a return to the Lord, and to do it in a way most likely to bring results. The Israelites understood prostitution; the men often went to pagan temples and participated in fertility rites with the prostitutes there. The Lord's comparisons were meaningful. *All* were implicated. Sometimes women—and men too—must sacrifice their feelings and refuse to take offense in the interest of the greater good, the welfare of all people.

When we do this, we find reassurance from our Lord in Isaiah 54:6-8: "Israel, you are like a young wife, deserted by her husband and deeply distressed. But the Lord calls you back to Him and says: 'For one brief moment I left you; with deep love I will take you back. I turned away angry for only a moment, but I will show you my love forever.' So says the Lord who saves you."

LET'S PRAY: Thank You, Lord, for saving us and for assuring us that Your love for us will never end. It's good to know that You will care for us as a mother nurses her child (Is. 60:16) and carry us in Your arms (Is. 66:12). Now nurture us so that we will be strong and healthy (Is. 66:14) and willing and able to do Your will. In Jesus' name. Amen.

The Prophets

I Want Your Love!

D o you remember this chant from your childhood days? Perhaps you've even repeated it:

"Latin is a language that is dead, dead, dead.
First it killed the Romans and now it's killing me."

Sometimes people have the same sentiments about the Old Testament. They see it as outdated, replaced by the New Testament. The long names and all the "begats" become roadblocks to understanding. The culture, the climate, and the concerns of the people seem alien to us today. The conclusion: life was so different then that none of this can possibly apply to me.

Reading the prophets will change your mind!

For example:

- In Amos 4, as well as today, we find women "who grow fat like the well-fed cows of Bashan, who mistreat the weak, oppress the poor, and demand that [their] husbands keep [them] supplied with liquor!"
- In Isaiah 3 we read about women of Jerusalem who "walk along with their noses in the air. They are always flirting. They take dainty little steps, and the bracelets on their ankles jingle."
- In Amos again we learn of people with winter homes and summer homes . . . houses decorated with ivory. Just like the pictures in today's home decorating magazines, perhaps?
- In Zechariah 10 people consult idols and fortune-tellers. Today we have astrology columns in newspapers and palm readers in hotels.
- In Obadiah 12-13 God tells the Edomites: "You should not have laughed at [My people] in their distress; you should not have entered the city of My

people to gloat over their suffering and seize their riches." It sounds like the aftermath of hurricanes and tornadoes today or the looting during power outages, doesn't it?

- And in Malachi the Lord accuses the people of viewing His altar as worthless and offering food for sacrifices that is not the very best. How many people nowadays fail to attend church regularly? How many give offerings that consist of leftovers rather than first fruits?

No, the people of Bible times were no different from now. Their homes may have been a different style, even tents in the wilderness at one time. Their language may have been Hebrew or Aramaic or Greek. Men may have been allowed several wives and concubines, but their sins were no different from ours, and God's expectations were always the same: "I want your constant love" (Hos. 6:6).

More specifically, "You must see that justice is done, and must show kindness and mercy to one another. Do not oppress widows, orphans, foreigners who live among you, or anyone else in need. And do not plan ways of harming one another" (Zech. 7:9-10).

Wouldn't it be great if everyone lived that way? The Lord tried to get His people back on the right path through the prophets, often illustrating their messages with drama and visual example to gain attention. Once a human hand appeared and wrote a message on the plaster wall of Nebuchadnezzar's palace. Another time Ezekiel acted out the forthcoming siege of Jerusalem, lying on his side for 390 days for the punishment of Israel and 40 for that of Judah. Then he cut off his hair and used a scale, sword, and fire to demonstrate what would happen to the people. Other "audiovisuals" included the breaking of pottery and having the prophets give their children names which carried a special message—such as "Unloved" or "Not-My-People" (Hos. 1).

The messages—and the prophets, as a result—were not always popular. Punishment was often the lot of the faithful. Daniel found himself in the lions' den, and Shadrach, Meshach, and Abednego were tossed into a fiery furnace, but God saved them—a miracle that surely tops modern science fiction!

Unfortunately, it was all to no avail! Finally in punishment, God's people were taken into exile—but not without hope, because ours is a loving God. As He assured them, so He promises us today, "I will make you my wife; I will be true and faithful; I will show you constant love and mercy and make you Mine forever" (Hos. 2:19). That's His timely message of timeless love—for them and for us!

LET'S PRAY: Dear Lord, thank You for the timeliness of the prophets and for Your assurance through them that You are ours forever. As You emphasized through Hosea, "You are our God" (2:23). All praise and glory and honor be Yours. In Jesus' name. Amen.

Evangelism

I Have Good News!

*I*n the television show "The Millionaire," the main character gave away a million dollars each week to someone with a special problem or need. That indeed was good news for the recipient!

Today millions of people regularly (and usually fruitlessly) buy lottery tickets in the hope of receiving thousands of dollars. Others vie for spots on TV game shows to win money and prizes. In every case, the winner immediately sets off to tell friends the good news! For most Americans, unexpected money is synonymous with "good news," and we want everyone to know about it.

During a lesson on evangelism, a Sunday school student had a different reaction, however. Asked by his teacher what he would do if someone visited their class and gave each student a $10 bill, the boy responded, "I'd hide it. If I told anyone about it, someone might take it away from me!"

Obviously, that wasn't the answer the teacher expected! As a result, she changed her approach and talked to the class about the Gift that no one can take away from them. Originally, she had planned to make the point that we have something worth far more than $10 or $1,000 or even $1,000,000. We have a Savior who loves us so much that He was willing to give His life so that we can have life eternal just by believing in Him.

And if we really *do* believe, then we have the best GOOD NEWS in the world . . . Good News that we will *want* to share with *everyone*.

It was women who first learned the Good News of Christ's resurrection. Twice in Matthew they were told to go and tell. Imagine their feelings as they arrived at the tomb: "Suddenly there was a violent earthquake; an angel of the Lord came down from heaven, rolled the stone away, and sat on it. His appearance was like lightning, and his clothes were white as snow. . . . The angel spoke to the women. 'You must not be afraid,' he said. 'I know you are looking for Jesus, who was crucified. He is not here; He has been raised, just as He said. Come here and see the place where He was lying. Go quickly, now, and tell His disciples' " (28:2-3, 5-6).

Imagine their joy. How they must have hurried! And then they saw Him!

How would you react? Would you be afraid . . . happy . . . speechless? The women "came up to Him, took hold of His feet, and worshiped Him." Christ understood their mixed feelings and immediately sought to put them at ease. "Do not be afraid," He said. But then He repeated the angel's words: "Go and tell . . ." (28:9-10). That was their commission, just as it is ours today.

Are we ready? Or are we like the foolish virgins of Matthew 25? Five of the 10 did not take any extra oil for their lamps and were unprepared when the bridegroom finally came. If we want our testimony to shine, to light the way for others to come to the Lord, we must be prepared through prayer and familiarity with God's Word.

The New Testament is our primary source of knowledge about the Savior and the development of the early Christian church. The first three books of the New Testament tell the story of Jesus from the same point of view, even reporting major events in the same order, while John, the fourth gospel, supplements their accounts with a different perspective and additional details.

Matthew, the tax collector, wrote especially for the Jewish people. His goal was to demonstrate that Christ is the promised Messiah. Therefore, he traced Christ's lineage back to Abraham and showed how Christ fulfilled the Old Testament prophecies. Because the Jews expected God to send an earthly ruler, Matthew made 32 references to the "kingdom of God" to help them understand that it is a heavenly kingdom.

How thankful we should be that Christ was not just an earthly king! If that were the case, we would have no hope of heaven. As it is, we are rich! Sophie Tucker once said, "I have been rich and I have been poor, and rich is better." Yes, riches on earth are nice, but we have the best—the riches of heaven—and that's Good News worth telling!

LET'S PRAY: Thank You, dear Lord, for Your gift of eternal life. Please strengthen our faith and understanding of Your love so that we will be moved to freely share Your Good News. In Jesus' name. Amen.

Worry

Don't Be Afraid

*E*very year one million Americans have a heart attack. Eight million have ulcers. Five million doses of tranquilizers are prescribed annually. No wonder people call this "the Age of Anxiety."

Yet, stress and anxiety have always been with us—even in Bible times. We read about one very worried father in Mark. And since Mark, like the other three gospels, is the story of Jesus' life on earth, we also find out *what Jesus did* about that father's worries.

What Jesus did about it . . . Those five words are a good summary of the Book of Mark. This is an action book reporting the *works* of Christ. It features 18 miracles and only 4 parables.

The author was Jewish by birth. His Hebrew name was John, but his Roman name was Mark. Since the gospel bears Mark's Latin name, some scholars feel that Mark wrote it for the Romans. A companion of the apostles, Mark was the son of Mary, an important member of the church at Jerusalem. The disciples often gathered at her home.

Undoubtedly they often talked there about all the people Jesus had healed . . . including the daughter of Jairus, an official of a synagogue near the Sea of Galilee. One day while Jesus was speaking to a large crowd at the lakeside (Mark 5), Jairus ran up, threw himself at Jesus' feet, and begged the Lord to come to his house and heal his daughter.

Jesus started off with Jairus, undoubtedly moving slowly because of the size of the crowd that accompanied them. It was at this time that the woman with the flow of blood touched Jesus and was healed. While Christ was talking with her, messengers came from

Jairus's home to inform him that his daughter had died. Christ ignored the message, telling Jairus, "Don't be afraid, only believe."

Leaving the crowd behind, and taking only Peter, James, and John with Him, Jesus went immediately to Jairus's home. All was in confusion there, and everyone was crying and wailing because of the child's death.

"Why are you crying? The child is not dead; she is only sleeping!" Christ told them. The response was not joy, but ridicule!

Jesus simply ignored their taunts and took the parents and his disciples to the child's room. There He took her by the hand and said, "Little girl, I tell you to get up." And she did!

So often we also cannot believe the extent of God's power and love. So often He tells us, "Do not be afraid; do not worry," and yet we do. We totally forget His words in Matthew:

> "Do not be worried about the food and drink you need in order to stay alive, or about clothes for your body. . . . Look at the birds flying around: they do not plant seeds, gather a harvest and put it in barns; yet your Father in heaven takes care of them! Aren't you worth much more than birds? Can any of you live a bit longer by worrying about it?" (6:25-27).

The answer of course is *no*, but we keep trying anyway, refusing simply to trust. When we read the Bible, we see over and over and over again how marvelously God cared for those who were faithful to Him. Sometimes we say, "If I had lived then . . . if I had actually seen a miracle, it would be so easy to trust."

We are more fortunate than that. We have the entire Bible where all the miracles are recorded for us. In particular, we have the Book of Mark, where we meet Jesus, the Man of action, the God of love. In response, let's simply say with Paul, "For me to live is Christ and to die is gain" (Phil. 1:21 RSV).

LET'S PRAY: Dear Lord, our nation relies on pills for peace and alcohol for escape. Help us to fully know and widely share the fact that You are the only real answer to worry and stress and the only sure hope for personal peace. In Jesus' name. Amen.

Generosity

She Gave All She Had

L ittle Debbie could hardly wait for her favorite aunt, who had just arrived, to sit down. Climbing onto her aunt's lap, Debbie whispered excitedly, "Do you know what I am getting Daddy for his birthday?" Without waiting for an answer, Debbie continued, "A pair of slippers!"

"And who's going to pay for them?" her aunt asked.

"Oh, Daddy will give me the money," Debbie answered confidently. Debbie's aunt smiled to herself, thinking about the irony of her brother's paying for his own birthday present.

The situation isn't as strange as it may seem, though, for we do the same thing regularly. Whenever we give a gift to the Lord, we too are offering Him that which already belongs to Him, for everything we have is a gift from the Lord. How thankful we can be that the Lord welcomes and accepts our gifts. He not only provides the means but blesses us for sharing.

From Mark's gospel, we learn what the Lord expects of us—and what He promises in return. The widow with her mite set the example for us:

As Jesus sat near the temple treasury, he watched the people as they dropped in their money. Many rich men dropped in a lot of money; then a poor widow came along and dropped in two little copper coins, worth about a penny. He called his disciples together and said to them, "I tell you that this poor widow put more in the offering box than all the others. For the others put in what they had to spare of their riches; but she, poor as she is, put in all she had—she gave all she had to live on" (12:41-44).

Perhaps that widow remembered another

woman—the poor widow of a prophet in 2 Kings 4:1-7. A man to whom this woman's husband had owed money wanted to take away her two sons as slaves in payment for the debt. All she had in her house was a small jar of oil.

When she told the prophet Elisha her problem, he sent her to the neighbors to borrow as many empty jars as she could. Then he directed the woman and her sons to close the door and start pouring oil into the jars. When all were filled, the olive oil stopped flowing. "Now," said Elisha, "sell the olive oil and pay all your debts, and there will be enough money left over for you and your sons to live on."

Obviously, the widow in Matthew who gave the mite also understood the lesson Jesus taught in Mark 10:28-31. There the disciples were reminding the Lord that they had left everything and followed Him.

In response, Christ gave this great promise: "Anyone who leaves home or brothers or sisters or mother or father or children or fields for me and for the gospel will receive much more in this present age. He will receive a hundred times more houses, brothers, sisters, mothers, children and fields . . . and in the age to come he will receive eternal life."

The widow trusted and she gave accordingly. The Lord expects the same of us. He loves a cheerful giver, and He Himself sets the example. He gave His life for our eternal welfare, and He richly provides for us in this world. True, there may be persecutions and problems, but the blessings will far outnumber them because we can't outgive the Lord. He is the Master of multiplication!

We see proof whenever we pass a field of corn. For each kernel planted and nurtured, the farmer knows that 120 days later, the Lord will bring forth a stalk with two ears of a thousand kernels each. That's 2,000 for one!

So also we can be sure the Lord will bless us, both now and in eternity.

LET'S PRAY: Dear Lord, thank You for giving us

our daily bread, and thank You for assuring us throughout the Bible that You will always care for us. Teach
us to give our all with as much faith as the widow gave
her mite. In Jesus' name. Amen.

Trust

No One Told the Neighbors

Our Jewish friends are still anticipating the birth of a Messiah. How would you react if a teenage Jewish girl in your neighborhood announced tomorrow, "I am pregnant by the Holy Spirit"?

You probably would think, "Wow, she's really cooked up a tall tale to cover her indiscretion!" And that's most likely what Mary's relatives and neighbors thought when they learned she was going to have a baby.

When the angel appeared to Mary with the news, Luke tells us that "Mary was deeply troubled by the angel's message" (1:29). She had good reason to be troubled. She lived in a land where the laws allowed unwed mothers to be stoned to death.

"I am a virgin. How, then, can this be?" Mary asked the angel. Joseph, her fiancé, had similar questions when he learned about Mary's pregnancy, but he was a nice person. As Matthew reports (1:19), "Joseph was a man who always did what was right, but he did not want to disgrace Mary publicly; so he made plans to break the engagement privately." That's when the angel appeared to Joseph, and consequently Joseph "married Mary, as the angel of the Lord had told him to" (1:24).

But no angel appeared to the neighbors or the relatives! How they must have gossiped! A Middle East missionary surmises that this is the reason Mary and Joseph did not plan to stay with relatives in Bethlehem but instead sought lodging at the inn when they arrived there for the census. Although hospitality to relatives, even the most distant relatives, was the rule of the land, Mary and Joseph would not have been welcome in the homes of family members because Joseph had not had Mary put to death. He had not even refused to marry her!

Arriving at the inn, they found no room—not even a tiny corner for a woman about to give birth to a child. Instead, the young couple was sent to a stable, most likely a cave in a hillside where shepherds drove their flocks for protection from the elements.

In those cold, dark surroundings, the Savior of the world made His appearance on earth. It was a birthplace far different from the warm, cozy manger settings portrayed in our Christmas pageants . . . settings enhanced by clean, sweet-smelling hay and illumined with lovely colored lights. Out of love for us, Christ humbled Himself from the moment of His birth. How grateful we should be! How often we should echo the words of Mary's Magnificat: "My heart praises the Lord; my soul is glad because of God my Savior, for He has remembered me, His lowly servant!" (1:46-55).

In complete trust, Mary had ultimately responded to the angel's first message to her, saying, "I am the Lord's servant; may it happen to me as you have said." The dictionary defines trust as "confident reliance on the integrity, honesty, veracity, or justice of another." Mary committed herself into the care of the Lord, and she was not disappointed.

Throughout Luke and the other three gospels, we see evidence of God's guiding and protecting hand over the young family. For instance, the Lord provided physical and emotional support through the songs of angels at the birth; the testimony of Simeon and Anna, the prophetess at the dedication of the child in the temple; and through the angel's warning to flee to Egypt. And who will ever forget Christ's own loving provision for His mother 33 years later as He hung on the cross!

Women today can also rely on the Lord for guidance and support, and they can be sure their trust will not be in vain. The gospel of Luke is especially reinforcing for women. Perhaps because the author was the "beloved physician," a person deeply concerned about people and their needs, this book contains more information about the role of women in the ministry of Jesus than any of the other gospels.

During His life on earth, Christ healed, counseled, taught, and encouraged women. He does the same for us today. The proof positive is Christ's gift of His own life for ours.

LET'S PRAY: Dear Lord, we are so grateful that You came to earth to assure us of forgiveness for our sins and eternal life with You in heaven. We praise You for setting us free, and we trust You, knowing that through faith in You, we are not only saved, but we are holy and righteous before the Lord all the days of our lives.[1] In Jesus' name. Amen.

Bible Study

Letter from the Lord

What warms you like a fire, nourishes you like milk and meat, lights your pathway through life, hits you with its truth "like a hammer that shatters rock," is sharper than a two-edged sword, reflects your true self like a mirror, builds you up and gives you the blessings of God?[1]

Perhaps you're thinking, "Nothing can do all those things! What kind of hoax is this? If someone or something could accomplish all that, it would be more valuable than gold, more desirable than jewels, more sought after than the fountain of youth."

It's no hoax. There *is* an answer to this riddle. Most people in the U.S. have a copy, sometimes several copies. But in many homes, it sits on a shelf gathering dust. The answer, of course, is the Bible, God's Word, His written message to us.

Our Lord knows the value of written communication. He Himself wrote the Ten Commandments on tablets of stone. In Habakkuk, He urges, "Write down clearly on tablets what I reveal to you so it can be read at a glance. Put it in writing" (2:2-3).

Even in this age of electronic communication, letters from friends and relatives mean so much to us. How eagerly we go to the mailbox each day to see if anyone has written to us. How upset we are if the mail is late. And what value we place on letters from famous people! Recipients not only show them to everyone—they may even sell them. Newspapers often carry stories about auctions where collectors pay thousands of dollars for old letters written by U.S. presidents, movie stars, and others. Yet we ignore the greatest collection of all letters—letters that carry the seal of our Lord, letters that can introduce us to the source of eternal life, letters that assure us we are never alone or forgotten.

For women, this unfamiliarity with God's Word, this failure to read it regularly is particularly tragic, because there was a time when women were not encouraged to study the Scriptures. The Jews at the time of Christ did not even think it necessary to educate women. Only men studied with the scribes. Only men gathered for philosophical discussions at the gates of cities and in places of business and trade.

But Christ changed all that! It happened at the home of Martha and Mary. When Jesus came to visit these two sisters, Mary "sat at the Lord's feet listening to what he said. But Martha was distracted by all the preparations that had to be made. She came to him and asked, 'Lord, don't you care that my sister has left me to do the work by myself? Tell her to help me!' 'Martha, Martha,' the Lord answered, 'you are worried and upset about many things, but only one thing is needed. Mary has chosen what is better, and it will not be taken away from her' " (10:39-42 NIV).

So we too must choose the right thing! Thanks to Christ, we can daily turn to God's Word for comfort and companionship, for guidance and inspiration . . . perhaps in the morning before other family members are awake, perhaps during a devotion period before or after a meal, perhaps at night as we prepare to retire.

What joy to know that the Lord of the universe is speaking to us through the words of the Bible . . . speaking to us in our own language. Not everyone is so blessed. In more than 2,000 cultures, people do not have the Word of the Lord in their own tongue. But most of us who live in North America do.

In fact, most of us have it in many versions! For ease of reading, we can choose the *Good News Bible*. For beauty and elegance of expression, we can select the King James version. For modern applications, we can use paraphrases like *Phillips Modern English Bible* or the Cotton Patch version. For comparison and understanding, we can purchase books with as many as eight translations printed in parallel columns. The choice is ours. If we fail to act, we are the losers, for in His Word is peace and hope and love.

If the Lord were to appear before us right now and speak to us, we would treasure His words—every one of them! Since He does speak to us now through His Word, let's open the pages of our Bible daily and listen like Mary!

LET'S PRAY: Thank You, Lord, for understanding our need to read and reread Your words to us. Thank You for the gift of the Scriptures and for all who have translated them so we may read Your message for ourselves. Help us treasure the Bible and turn to it daily for peace and support and direction. In Jesus' name. Amen.

The Trinity

Three-in-One—the Total God

A rtists have struggled for years to portray the triune God. Three persons but one God is a difficult concept to picture—and to understand. A common symbol is the triangle. An altar parament in a chapel for retarded persons uses an apple because it takes three parts—the skin, flesh, and seeds (or core)—to make the apple. Some teachers hold three matches together; when lit, they burn with one flame.

Luke used three parables to demonstrate the work of Father, Son, and Holy Spirit.

Referred to by Paul as "the beloved physician," Luke was a learned man with a warm interest in people. The author of both Luke and Acts, he understood not only how to write but also how to select material. His accuracy has been supported by archeologists, and his gospel gives us "the fullest life-story of Jesus we possess."[1]

Writing for Gentile Christians, Luke focused on Christ as the Savior of the world. As Luther said, "Luke goes back farther and purposes, as it were, to make Christ the common property of all nations. For that reason he carried His genealogy back to Adam. In this way he wishes to show that this Christ is not only for the Jews, but also for Adam and his posterity, that is, for all people in all the world."[2]

"All people" includes women, and Luke, more than any of the other gospel writers, emphasizes the role of women in the life of Jesus. He preserves the inspired hymns of Elizabeth and Mary as they are awaiting the birth of John and Jesus. And he even includes a parable about a woman in his trio of parables which theologians view as an explanation of the work of the Father, Son, and Holy Spirit.

They are found in chapter 15, which is in the words of one commentator, "the golden center of this Gospel, revealing in a wonderful way the love of the Savior for the lost and condemned sinner."[3]

The first is the parable of the Good Shepherd who has 100 sheep. Yet, when he loses one of them, he leaves the 99 and searches for the lost sheep. In the same way, Jesus, the Son, calls to us, both men and women, when we stray—and eventually leads us to our home in heaven.

The role of the Father is illustrated in the parable of the prodigal son. When the wayward son returns home, the father forgives him and lovingly welcomes him back. So also our heavenly Father, who created us and preserves us in this life, will someday welcome us and all believers into our heavenly home with Him.

The parable of the lost coin illustrates the work of the Holy Spirit. Here Scripture describes a woman who has lost one of her 10 coins. "She lights a lamp, sweeps her house, and looks carefully everywhere until she finds it. When she finds it, she calls her friends and neighbors together, and says to them, 'I am so happy I found the coin I lost. Let us celebrate!' " (15:8-9).

Imagine then what celebration there is in heaven when one sinner repents! Just as the woman swept the house, so God's Spirit cleanses and illumines our hearts. Just as she continued to search until she found the coin, so the Spirit of the Lord does not give up on us throughout our life on earth. It's a wise woman (or man), however, who recognizes the folly of assuming there will be time for a deathbed conversion.

One thing is obvious in all three parables: our Lord *loves* us! Our Lord not only creates and preserves us, but He also guides, encourages, and protects us through the three persons of His Being. He cares for us as humans, as individuals, as women/men. His provision for us is *total*—and He who is our one God is the *total* answer to all our needs.

LET'S PRAY: Lord, we don't really understand how You can be three persons in one, but we believe it! Thank You, Father, for creating us. Thank You, Jesus, for shepherding us through this life and for loving us enough to die for us. Thank You, Holy Spirit, for teaching us and leading us to faith. We look forward to learning the mystery of Your unity when You call us to our eternal home with You. In Jesus' name. Amen.

Home Missions

I Want to Go to Africa

*H*ave you ever listened to a foreign missionary describe the excitement of moving to a faraway land, learning a new language and new customs, and then sharing Christ with people who have never heard of the Savior?

As a child, most of us have probably dreamed of traveling to a primitive land to tell the "natives" about Jesus. For Joyce Danforth of Ceylon, India, that desire surfaced as an adult, because that's when she became a Christian. Fired with enthusiasm for the Lord, this excited new believer prayed, "Why did you let me get married, Lord? I want to go to Africa and be a missionary, but I can't because of my family."

The Lord showed her that He wanted her to be a missionary right where she lives. She accepted the challenge, and through her, many people in India have been brought to the Lord.

In his gospel John shares the story of another woman who was a home missionary, the Samaritan woman at the well. She is one of the first missionaries in the Bible.

When Jesus was returning to Galilee from a visit to Judea, He and His disciples stopped at Jacob's well in Samaria. It was noon, and while the disciples were in town buying food, a woman came to draw water.

Christ asked her to give Him a drink also. She was shocked, because Jews normally would not use the same cups and bowls that Samaritans did. Jesus responded, "If you knew the gift of God and who it is that asks you for a drink, you would have asked him and he would have given you living water" (4:10 NIV).

Living water? That really aroused her curiosity!

This water gives eternal life, Christ explained, and whoever drinks of it will never be thirsty again!

You can imagine her response: "Sir, give me this water so that I won't get thirsty and have to keep coming here to draw water" (4:15 NIV).

Drawing water and carrying it home was hard work, but there most likely were other reasons for this woman's interest. As Christ soon revealed, she had been married five times and was now living with a man who was not her husband. Undoubtedly the other women of the village looked down on her, and she may have come to the well at noonday to avoid them and escape their taunts.

In true Christ-like fashion, it was to this unlikely candidate, this sinner, that our Lord made His first direct announcement that He is the Messiah. "I who speak to you am he" the Savior informed her as the two discussed true worship (4:26 NIV).

Leaving her water jar behind in her eagerness to share her discovery, she hurried back to her village "and said to the people there, 'Come, see a man who told me everything I ever did' " (4:28-29 NIV).

They came—and they believed.

Do we follow her example? Do we share the Good News with our family and our friends? Do we urge them, "Come to church with me and meet Christ"—or "Come to Bible study at my house and learn of the Savior of the world"?

If He's your friend, you'll be proud to introduce Him to all who touch your life. As the Samaritan woman demonstrated, you don't have to go to Africa to have the joy of being a missionary.

LET'S PRAY: Dear Jesus, make us "bubblers," fountains overflowing with the Good News of Your love for us. Help us guide others to the joy which can be found only through faith in You. In Your most holy name, we pray. Amen.

Faith

I Believe

What is true faith? The dictionary defines it as "confidence in a person, statement, or thing as trustworthy"—or more simply, it says faith is "trust."

A story about an accomplished daredevil illustrates the meaning more vividly. After several successful feats, he has decided to string a wire across Niagara Falls and push a wheelbarrow over it. If you have seen his other accomplishments, you may say, "I believe he can do it," but that's not faith. Faith is getting into the wheelbarrow and letting him push you across.

Likewise, complete trust in God means sitting in God's wheelbarrow and letting Him do the pushing in your life. The Bible is full of people who did just that. Noah built the ark before there was any water to necessitate it. Moses left Egypt without knowing where God would lead him and the Israelites. Daniel prayed to God instead of the king, even though it meant being thrown into a den of lions.

But what about us today? So often we Christians have faith in the past and the future, but the present presents a problem. We believe that Jesus died on the cross years ago for our sins, and we believe that in the future we will live with Him in heaven—but what about trusting Him with our lives *now?* Do we have enough faith to risk it?

We *will* have if we confess with Martha, "Yes, Lord, . . . I do believe that You are the Messiah, the Son of God" (11:27). Martha made her beautiful confession of faith after the death of Lazarus, her brother.

The story is found in the Book of John. The goal of this fourth gospel is to help readers understand that

Jesus is just what Martha says: the promised Savior, the Son of God.

An eyewitness account of the life of Jesus, this book contains no parables but focuses on the deeds (the "signs") of Jesus. Unlike the other gospels, which had a missionary intent, this book strives to deepen the faith of believers. The author is John, the "disciple whom Jesus loved" (21:20), a member of Christ's inner circle, and the last of the 12 to die. John also wrote Revelation and the three letters of John.

Lazarus and his sisters, Mary and Martha, were also beloved friends of Jesus. When Christ arrived at their home four days after Lazarus had been buried, Martha said to Him, "If you had been here, Lord, my brother would not have died" (11:21).

Even though she at one time chose to work in the kitchen rather than sit at Christ's feet and learn, it is obvious in the 11th chapter of John that her faith has grown since then. Not only does she understand that Christ is the Savior, but she also is positive that those who believe in Christ "will rise to life on the last day" (11:24). In the case of her brother, she doesn't have to wait that long to see him again. Christ goes to the tomb with her, calls to Lazarus to come out—and he appears!

The result? Many believed.

And what about us? Is our faith as sure as Martha's? It should be, for we not only have the proof of this miracle but the entire record of Christ's life. We know His deeds, His love, His promises, His resurrection, and His ascension. With such proof, who can doubt?

LET'S PRAY: Dearest Jesus, we confess with Martha that You are the Promised Savior, the Son of God. We know You love us too, and we trust You. We want to ride in Your wheelbarrow and go wherever You take us so that Your will may be done. Amen.

Talents

God Doesn't Do a Bum Job

"**N**umber your paper from one to three and list three of your talents," the speaker directed the audience.

From the back of the room, a little old lady called out, "But what if you don't have any?"

So often we think we have no talents because we define the word in terms of the abilities that the world idolizes: the ability to sing like an opera star, the ability to speak like a politician, or the ability to paint like a great artist.

Dorcas had no such problem. She recognized her talents, and she used them. Her story is told in Acts. This book describes how the Holy Spirit led the early Christians to share the Good News of Jesus—first in Jerusalem, then throughout Palestine, and finally among the countries surrounding the Mediterranean Sea. A continuation of Luke, the Acts of the Apostles focuses on the missionary journeys of Paul, his arrest in Jerusalem, and imprisonment in Caesarea and Rome.

Peter, like Paul, traveled everywhere for the Lord. It was in Joppa that he learned of Tabitha (or Dorcas, as she was called in Greek). She had just died, and there was much mourning, for Dorcas had "spent all her time doing good and helping the poor" (9:36).

As Peter entered the upstairs room where her body lay, he was besieged by weeping widows who showed him all the coats and clothing Dorcas had made for them. Peter sent them out of the room, then knelt and prayed. Next he turned to the body and said, "Tabitha, get up!" She opened her eyes and sat up. Peter then called in the people and presented her alive. As word of the miracle spread throughout the country, many believed in Christ.

As we use our talents, we also can open doors for Christ—perhaps, like Dorcas, by sewing or caring for the poor, perhaps by lending a listening ear, preparing a meal for a bereaved family, pushing a wheelchair, holding an office in a church organization, teaching children, being a mother, praying with or for others, touching, contributing, witnessing, or . . . what are your talents? Can you name three of them?

Does that question trouble you? Do you feel it's sinful, a sign of pride, to admit you have talents? We have no talents because we deserve them; rather, they are the gifts of a loving Lord. It is not exhibiting pride but praising God to admit this.

Sometimes we do such stupid things and feel so idiotic that we honestly believe we are worthless and have no talents. However, what we are really saying then is: "Hey, Lord, when You made me, You did a bum job!" But God doesn't do a bum job. As a bumper sticker declares: God doesn't make junk.

Sometimes other people convince us we have no talents. Enrico Caruso, probably the greatest tenor who ever lived, once was told by a music teacher, "You can't sing. You have no voice at all." The noted author Louisa May Alcott was informed by an editor that her writing lacked popular appeal. Walt Disney, F. W. Woolworth, Thomas Edison, Beethoven, and Einstein had similar experiences, but that didn't stop them.

Perhaps you think you are too old to use your talents or discover new ones. Margaret Chase Smith was first elected to the Senate at age 49, Golda Meir became prime minister of Israel at age 71, and Grandma Moses didn't even begin painting until age 76!

With God as the giver, talents are unlimited by age, station in life, or the fact that we are "poor, sinful beings." With God, nothing is impossible, and He will prove it daily in our lives if we let Him.

Michelangelo, the noted sculptor, once said his goal was to bring out the angel in the marble. If we trust the Lord, He will do the same in us so that we can use our talents to bring out the angel in others.

LET'S PRAY: Dear Lord, thank You for seeing possibilities in us that we do not realize exist. Thank You for never giving up on us, for renewing us daily to serve You with all the talents and abilities You have given us. Help us realize our potential so that we may accomplish the purpose for which You have placed us on earth. In Jesus' name. Amen.

Careers

Profits Doubled

M ary Baim took over a failing chain of home re-modeling stores, and within two years the profits doubled and sales reached $20 million.

When teachers said they needed something other than gold stars to reward their students' good work, Kay Fredericks created Stinky Stickers, with scents ranging from peanut butter to old socks. Her company has sold over a billion!

When her father and his business partner died within two weeks of each other, 22-year-old Victoria Jackson took over their diesel engine company and soon recorded a 185 percent increase in sales.[1]

Modern magazines and newspapers are full of success stories like these about 20th-century career women. Although women are working outside the home in far greater numbers today, there were also career women in Bible times. Besides the religious and political leaders (prophetesses and queens), the Old Testament mentions women who were midwives, shepherdesses, nursemaids, doorkeepers, builders, and weavers. In the New Testament, Priscilla was a partner with her husband in tentmaking; and Lydia, Paul's first European convert and the most famous business-woman in the Bible, was a seller of purple cloth.

Paul met Lydia on his second missionary journey. She lived in Philippi, an important center of trade located on the main Roman road between Europe and Asia. Originally from Thyatira, a community noted for its dyeing of yarn and fabrics, Lydia sold purple goods and possibly the dye itself. The dye may have come from the madder root, which grew abundantly in that area or from a species of shellfish found in the Mediterranean Sea. Since purple (the word also included various hues of red) was a symbol of majesty and wealth and was very costly, Lydia's customers would have been people of means, and her business undoubtedly was profitable.

Apparently there were not enough Jews in Philippi to support a synagogue, so the faithful gathered for worship at a site on the banks of the Gangites River outside the city gates. The group, mostly women, included Lydia. When Paul and his companions joined them for prayer on the Sabbath, he shared the news of Jesus Christ, and Lydia believed.

As a result, she and all the people of her house were baptized. Scholars surmise that she was a widow whose household included her children and servants. After the Baptism, Lydia invited Paul, Silas, and Timothy to stay in her home, and it became a gathering place for believers.

In the days to follow, Paul met a woman whose career was not of her choice. She was "a slave girl who had a spirit by which she predicted the future" (16:16 NIV). She began following Paul and shouting, "These men are servants of the Most High God, who are telling you the way to be saved" (16:17 NIV).

When this went on for days, Paul became frustrated by the turmoil it created. He may also have felt that these words from a fortune-teller would give listeners a wrong impression of the origin of his message. Therefore he cast out her evil spirit, freeing her from its control but incurring the wrath of her owners because their source of profit was gone. Their complaints sent Paul and Silas to jail for a night, but even that provided an opportunity to share the Good News of Christ.

Through faith in Christ, all women today are also set free for good works, and following the example set by Lydia, they can use the resources which they earn to benefit the kingdom of God.

Today over 70 percent of women born during the baby boom from 1946 to 1955 are in the labor force, and authorities expect that figure to reach 80 percent by the mid-90s. Because of modern economics, housekeeping conveniences, and societal attitudes, it is unlikely that two-career families will decrease in the foreseeable future. The challenge to women, therefore—and to men—is to manage their lives in such a way that the Lord never takes second place in their priorities, for all the money in the world, all the fame and success, and all the accomplishments of this life will mean nothing in eternity without faith in Jesus Christ.

LET'S PRAY: Dear Lord, thank You for believers like Paul who are willing to endure personal hardship and even imprisonment to share Your freedom with men and women of all walks of life. Help us keep our priorities straight so that You come first in all we do. Turn our work, both in the home and in the marketplace, into a double profit, a double benefit, by giving us additional resources for Your ministry and additional opportunities to share Your Good News. In Jesus' name. Amen.

Christian Service

Strengthen One Another

Will the day come when we don't need people? One is almost tempted to take that question seriously after reading stories of the increasing use of robots and other mechanical aides.

Even in the early 1970s some medical centers were turning to automation to eliminate staff positions. A Virginia hospital, for instance, installed 60 carts to deliver meals and supplies to patients on six floors. Each cart buzzes the elevator electronically, glides aboard, chooses the proper floor, and gets off. After someone there unloads its contents, each cart returns to the basement, waits for its trays to be removed, proceeds to the cart wash for sterilization, and then lines up for another load. The carts allow 16 people to do the work of 45 porters.

Today dolls and cars talk, computers compose music, and airplanes fly on automatic pilot. What's lacking, though, is the human dimension—the love, the caring, the concern, and the doing because a need is perceived.

How many churches, for instance, are blessed because volunteers and retired individuals do whatever needs doing! In one white frame country church in Wisconsin, a gray-haired couple washes the windows, changes the storm windows and screens, cleans the kitchen cupboards—and feels blessed to be busy. The congregation feels grateful to have them.

Most social service agencies could not continue without volunteers. At one large facility for retarded persons, over 5,000 people annually donate more than 70,000 hours of service. They write letters, take people for walks, perform in programs, and even give up their own Christmas Day to help the residents open their presents.

Paul likewise was grateful for the services of Phoebe. His chapter 16 postscript to the Letter to the Romans resembles a roll call of saints who were "helpers in Christ" to him, and the first to be mentioned is Phoebe.

In Luther's estimation, Romans is "the chief book of the New Testament and the purest Gospel, which is well worthy that a Christian should not only know it by heart, word for word, but daily use it as the daily bread of the soul; for you can never read and study it too often and too well, and the more you use it, the more precious does it become, and the better does it taste."[1]

Although Paul's parents were Jewish, he was a Roman citizen and hoped to visit Rome as a stepping stone to carrying the Gospel to Spain. The author of 14 New Testament letters, Paul wrote to the Romans to prepare them for his visit, to unify the congregation there, and to establish it as a base for the westward spread of Christianity. Little did he know that when he arrived, he would be in chains.

His theme is that God puts people right with Himself through faith in Jesus Christ, who sets them free and makes them God's friends. In gratitude, believers offer themselves "as a living sacrifice to God, dedicated to His service" (12:1).

"Conquer evil with good," Paul tells them (12:21). "Try to do what everyone considers to be good" (12:17). "Love one another warmly . . . and be eager to show respect for one another" (12:10). "Share your belongings with your needy fellow Christians, and open your homes to strangers" (12:13).

Judging from the letter's postscript, Phoebe and a number of other women did exactly that. Considering some of Paul's statements about the role of women in other letters, it's interesting that Paul here identifies several women as fellow workers who are well known among the apostles.

Historians believe that Phoebe carried Paul's letter to Rome. A "diakonos" (officer) in the church at Cenchreae, Phoebe is also described as a "prostatis"—an advocate who stands by in case of need. "Give her any help she may need from you," Paul tells the Romans, "for she has been a great help to many people, including me" (16:2 NIV).

That's what Christian service is: caring for others, especially those of the same household of faith. As Paul says, it's "summed up in this one rule: 'Love your neighbor as yourself' " (13:9 NIV). Or put another way: "Always aim at those things that bring peace and that help strengthen one another" (14:19).

LET'S PRAY: Dear Lord, help us also to live not for ourselves but for You and those whom You would have us serve. In Jesus' name. Amen.

Orderliness

Friday Was Cleaning Day

D o you remember when homemakers washed clothes on Monday, ironed on Tuesday, mended on Wednesday, went calling on Thursday, cleaned on Friday, shopped on Saturday, and went to church and relaxed on Sunday? In those "good ol' days," spring and fall housecleaning—dreaded by everyone—was also a "must." Life, however, had a simplicity and orderliness because everything had a time and place.

In our more complex modern age, order still has its place. Programming a computer requires a step-by-step progression, or the output will not be usable. Airplanes require regular and precise maintenance check-ups, or they may crash during a flight. Business people take classes in time management to systematize their lives.

Paul identified the ongoing need for order when he wrote to the Corinthians, "Everything must be done in a proper and orderly way" (1 Cor. 14:40).

Corinth, the capital of Achaia (now Greece), was a commercial center with nearly half a million inhabitants. Because it was located on an isthmus, most of the traffic between the East and the West passed through its gates. As a result, it was a cosmopolitan city of great wealth and culture—as well as widespread immorality.

With the inhabitants coming from many lands, the people were exposed to varied philosophies and religions, including temple prostitution. Historians tell us that 1,000 women were kept in a huge temple dedicated to Aphrodite (Venus), the Greek goddess of love. So unsavory was the city's reputation that the word "Corinthianize," meaning to practice extreme sexual license and self-indulgence, was coined.

Paul established the church at Corinth on his second missionary journey. It was a logical location. From there, the Gospel would likely be carried by travelers to many parts of the world. However, with its mixed membership of Jews and Gentiles, both rich and poor, the congregation soon found itself involved in numerous conflicts. Paul wrote his two letters to the Corinthians to resolve some of these disagreements.

The letters emphasize peace and love. No more beautiful description of love exists than in 1 Corinthians 13. This is to be the Christian way of life. God has called all of us to live in peace, Paul stresses (1 Cor. 7:15), and all that we do is to be done to God's glory (1 Cor. 10:31).

As always, Paul's goal is to spread the Good News. To accomplish this, he establishes two principles. Even though we have total freedom in Christ and are to be slaves to no one, Paul says that in order to save more people, believers should (1) follow the customs of their day (so long as they do not violate God's law) and (2) be willing to become all things to all people (1 Cor. 9:19-22).

He tells the Corinthians, therefore, that "any woman who prays or proclaims God's message in public worship" should have her head covered (1 Cor. 11:5-6). To do otherwise would be a disgrace to her husband because normally only the prostitutes walked in public without a head-covering.

Moreover, "as the Jewish Law says, [women] must not be in charge" during the Sabbath gatherings of the believers (1 Cor. 14:34). Apparently, New Testament worship services lacked the structure of synagogue ceremonies and the liturgies of today. People suggested hymns, spoke in tongues, and taught as they were inspired by the Holy Spirit. Properly attired prophetesses evidently could speak, but all other women were to keep quiet, and if they wanted to find out about something, they were to ask their husbands at home. A factor in Paul's enforcement of this rule was most likely the uneducated status of women at that time.

One woman who was a fluent instructor of the Gospel was Priscilla. With her husband, Aquila, she was a highly respected co-worker of Paul—so respected, in fact, that in his letters, Paul usually mentions her name before that of her husband's.

Formerly of Rome, the couple moved to Corinth when Emperor Claudius ordered all the Jews to leave Rome. Paul met them when he arrived in Corinth, and since they were tentmakers like himself, Paul stayed and worked with them. The church at Corinth met in their home. When Paul went on to Ephesus, they followed and hosted the new congregation there. Paul therefore closes his letter to the Corinthians with greetings also from Priscilla and Aquila.

Moving around as she and her husband did, helping in the family business, and still giving first priority to the Lord's work, Priscilla must have been well organized. Imagine having church in your home every Sunday. Probably most of us would clean not just on Friday but all week! Our goal, though, must be to "purify *ourselves* from everything that makes body or soul unclean and . . . be completely holy by living in reverence for God" (2 Cor. 7:1 emphasis added).

LET'S PRAY: Dearest Lord, You have taught us through Paul's letters to the Corinthians that "woman is not independent of man, nor is man independent of woman"(1 Cor. 11:11 NIV); You have brought us all into existence and given each of us spiritual gifts for Your purposes. Therefore help us work together so that, like Paul, we may "win as many as possible" for You (1 Cor. 9:19 NIV). In Jesus' name. Amen.

Freedom

Free to Be Me

A little girl and her mother were visiting a neighbor who had a beautiful collection of blown glass and Hummel figurines. The child had been forewarned that she was not to touch anything breakable. As she gazed in awe at delicate pieces, the child said, "Oh, Mother, just look at all those pretty no-no's!"

That's how some people view the life of a Christian—just one no-no after another:

- "Don't swear."
- "Don't steal."
- "Don't accuse anyone falsely."
- "Don't get drunk."
- "Don't desire another person's property."
- "Don't commit adultery."

Unfortunately, they never get beyond the prohibitions to the freedom. They assume that everything worldly, every enticement, everything that is fun is forbidden fruit to the Christian. Some believers also give that impression as they walk around with long faces and create measuring sticks for faith and behavior that do not appear in the Bible.

That's what was happening during the late A.D. 40s in Galatia (a Roman province covering a portion of modern-day Turkey). After Paul established churches there, the area was visited by other Jewish teachers who claimed that all believers—both Jews and Gentiles—must be circumcised. In other words, they were saying that eternal life can and must be earned by following rules of good conduct—that is, we can earn our way to heaven.

Deeply concerned, Paul reminded the Galatians that salvation is the gift of God: "A person is put right with God only through faith in Jesus Christ, never by doing what the Law requires" (2:16). This applies to women as well as men, he assures us. "There is no difference between Jews and Gentiles, between slaves and free men, between men and women; you are all one in union with Christ Jesus" (3:28).

To illustrate what freedom in Christ means, he compares the children of Hagar and Sarah. Children of a slave (Hagar) do not freely inherit their father's property. Their only recourse is to seek favor by obeying the Law, just as the Israelites at Mt. Sinai were under the Law. But that's impossible for us human beings, for we are naturally drawn to sin. But Isaac, the son of Sarah (the free woman), was the result of God's promise and the automatic heir of all his father's goods.

So we too, if we believe in Christ, the Promised Savior, are heirs of all God's good gifts. As Paul says, "Freedom is what we have—Christ has set us free!" (5:1). When we believe, Christ dwells in us; and when the Lord looks at us, He sees "the righteousness of Christ" and not the wrongness of our sins.

Yes, in Christ we are free, *really* free because we are forgiven—FREE TO BE YOU, FREE TO BE ME. Free of our sins, we are free to be the most that we possibly can be, free to use our God-given talents and abilities, free to fulfill the Lord's purpose for our lives!

In joyous gratitude, we become His servants . . . willingly and gladly—not because He forces us but because we *want* to serve Him. Filled with His Spirit, we enjoy the fruits of the Spirit: "love, joy, peace, patience, kindness, goodness, faithfulness, gentleness and self-control" (5:22 NIV).

In Christ, we are new people. No longer do we have a need to "escape" into a drunken stupor. No longer do we find it necessary to build ourselves up by pushing someone else down through gossip, name-calling, and accusations. No longer do we covet others' possessions, for we have all that is important. No longer do we view Christianity as a prison of no-no's; for thanks to Christ, who broke the lock, it's a treasure chest of blessings to which we happily say, "Yes, yes!"

LET'S PRAY: Blessed Savior, we are so grateful to You for opening the door to eternal life for us. Thank You for loving us enough to give Your life for us. Thank You for sending the Holy Spirit to guide us on our daily journey. We surrender our life to You and ask You to accomplish through us all that is Your will. In Your most holy name. Amen.

Marriage

Submit Yourselves to One Another

"**E**at, drink, and remarry." Those words embroidered on a pillow in an airport gift shop reflect the attitude of many modern adults. To them, marriage is temporary and rarely "for as long as you both shall live."

One national magazine carries a column entitled "Can This Marriage Be Saved?" Today lots of marriages do not last, and increasingly more couples are refusing to risk both marriage and divorce, so they live together without tying the knot. They see marriage as an uninsurable risk to be avoided. Speaking of a single neighbor, one young man said, "He died last month." Translation: the neighbor got married.

So what has given marriage such a bad name? Perhaps it's the fact that we live in a society that equates love with sex, joy with instant gratification, and permanence with "Dullsville." Surely, it's also the fact that most people don't understand and don't practice marriage according to God's standards in the Book of Ephesians.

Written from prison, Paul's Letter to the Ephesians encourages oneness in Christ—oneness in the church with Christ as the Head of the body, oneness in building with Christ as the cornerstone, and oneness in marriage by following the example of Christ and His bride, the church.

Such a marriage bears little resemblance to the old German "Herr Papa" tradition where the table-thumping head of the household ruled with a will of iron. He was the lord and master, and all the family had to do as he said. By contrast, Ephesians portrays marriage as a dual submission. Verse 5:21, in modern translations, is the topic sentence or theme of the section that follows on Christian marriage. It says: "Submit yourselves to one another because of your reverence for Christ."

The chapter then explains that the husband is the head of the house as Christ is the Head of the church. When the couple disagrees, the husband has the responsibility for decision-making; when leadership is required, the husband must lead. (Someone has to do it when there is no consensus, and Scripture designates the husband.)

Unfortunately, most theological discussions of marriage stop at this point, but Paul doesn't—for marital leadership is not dictatorship. Paul continues: "Husbands, love your wives, just as Christ loved the church and gave himself up for her. . . . Each one of you must love his wife as he loves himself" (5:25, 33 NIV). One pastor says he gets chills every time he reads that line, for he knows that he is humanly incapable of giving himself that fully.

What woman would not love a spouse who was willing to give his life for her and the children? What wife would not willingly honor and respect a husband who loved her that completely?

The beauty of this kind of Christian marriage, a union in which there is a dual submission, lies in the blessings it provides. Based on true commitment to each other, on caring as exemplified by Christ, Christian marriage offers the following:

- *Unfailing friendship*—someone with whom to share your innermost secrets, your hopes and dreams; someone you can trust; someone who trusts you; a companion who understands your joys and sorrows.
- *Mutual support*—someone who shares your goals, who remembers when you forget; someone who encourages and appreciates you as you develop your God-given talents; someone who both nurtures and needs you.
- *Real love*—someone who is faithful; someone who understands your need for togetherness and re-

spects your desire to be alone; someone whose presence offers peace and security; someone who is ready with the warmth of a touch, the security of a hug when you need it. (Researchers tell us that "hugging can help you live longer, protect you against illness, cure depression and stress, strengthen family relationships and even help you sleep without pills."[1])

- *Spiritual partnership*—someone with whom to pray, to study God's Word, to grow in faith; a co-worker in serving the Lord.
- *Opportunity for witnessing*—friends and neighbors will ask, "What makes your marriage so different?" You can answer, "We follow the example of our Lord. He gave His life so that we might live. Now we live to serve Him and each other."

LET'S PRAY: Lord, we thank You for establishing marriage as a lasting union and for setting the example through Your relationship with the church. Bless all who are married; help them face their daily challenges with patience and perseverance—and with consideration for their partner's needs. Give them happiness and a long life together. In Jesus' name. Amen.

Unity

Dealing with Differences Differently

Family feuds have taken many different forms over the years—from the 50-year battle between the Hatfields and the McCoys in the Kentucky hills a century ago to the popular TV show that ran for years and pitted two families against each other in a battle of wits. Even today family disagreements may culminate in a husband or wife killing the other or in a father or mother stealing the children from a former spouse.

Nor is the family of God without its share of disagreements. Congregations have split over doctrinal matters, fund drives, new hymnals, pastoral leadership, the color of paint, and dozens of other matters both serious and insignificant.

Paul also had to deal with quarrels in the fledgling Christian congregations of his day. At Corinth, the people split into factions, with one claiming to follow Paul, another Peter, another Apollos, and still another saying, "I follow Christ."

At Philippi, a problem arose between two women, Euodia and Syntyche. No reason is given for their disagreement. Some think it may have been personal; others suggest that it may have related to the church, which was meeting in homes. In his letter to the Philippians Paul encourages the women to resolve their differences: "I plead with Euodia and I plead with Syntyche to agree with each other in the Lord" (4:2 NIV). He asks Epaphroditus to help the women "for they have worked hard with me to spread the gospel" (4:3).

Throughout Philippians Paul urges peaceful, loving relationships. "Do everything without complaining or arguing," he says (2:14 NIV). He wants the Philippian Christians to shine "like stars lighting up the sky" (2:15).

Even though the letter was written from prison, Paul is full of joy and confidence. He stresses the importance of kindness, compassion and unity: "Make my joy complete by being like-minded, having the same love, being one in spirit and purpose" (2:2 NIV).

And what about us? Would our handling of disagreements in our parishes, our denominations and our church organizations make Paul and the Lord happy or sad? What does our approach to those who differ with us in the church say to the world? Does it help or hinder the Lord's cause?

The challenge is twofold when Christians face differences: (1) to maintain purity of doctrine and practice and (2) to demonstrate what the late Francis A. Schaeffer terms "a practicing, observable love," the oneness in Christ that all true Christians have. Schaeffer suggests that *before* differences arise between believers there should be conferences "to consider how true Christians can exhibit in practice a fidelity to the holiness of God and yet simultaneously exhibit in practice a fidelity to the love of God before a watching world"[1]

All too often in recent years, Christians have made the headlines repeatedly because of rifts in the ranks. Bad news sells, whether it's the defrocking of a pastor or the splitting of a church body. Given our human imperfections such situations will occur as long as this earth lasts. But what could change, through prayer and desire on our parts, is the way we deal with those differences.

As Schaeffer says, "Before a watching world an observable love in the midst of difference will show a difference between Christians' differences and other men's differences. The world may not understand what the Christians are disagreeing about, but they will very quickly understand the difference of our differences from the world's differences if they see us having our differences in an open and observable love on a practical level."[2]

The result will be less stress for us and, more importantly, greater credibility for the Lord. When one congregation becomes two, what if the parting were amicable? Instead of being competitive and jealous of other truly Christian churches in our community, what if we were to adopt Paul's attitude toward others who share the Word of God from different perspectives? He says: "It does not matter! I am happy about it—just so Christ is preached in every way possible, whether from right or wrong motives" (1:18).

When Christians deal with each other lovingly (or unlovingly), the world notices. The world views us as one body, but rarely do they see us treating each other that way. Christ prayed about this when He was here on earth and gave us the reason for showing love to sisters and brothers in the faith in the midst of differences: "Father! May they be in Us, just as You are in Me and I am in You. May they be one, so that the world will believe that You sent me. . . . and that You love them as You love me" (John 17:21-23).

That's not only Christ's prayer; it's His commandment. To each of us, He says: "As I have loved you, so you must love one another" (John 13:34 NIV).

LET'S PRAY: Loving Savior, help us love all who love You, even when it forces us to humble ourselves, even when it costs us something, even when it requires us to seek forgiveness or to forgive another while we still hurt inside. Thank You for setting the example of perfect love. Help us follow the pattern You have set so that others may know we are Christians by our love and through our love draw closer to You. We pray in Your most holy name. Amen.

Understanding

Give an Answer!

W hy is the sky blue?
What makes flowers grow?
How do birds fly?

What child has not asked these and dozens of other questions! And what parent has not struggled to answer simply and correctly!

But children aren't the only ones who ask questions—so do adults. It was no different in Christ's day. He and Paul were also besieged with questions, such as:

Shall we pay taxes?
Who gives you the authority to baptize?
May a man divorce his wife?

Some were asked by unbelievers who wanted to trap them; others came from Christians who were striving to grow from milk to meat in their spiritual diet.

Whatever the case, Paul and Jesus answered! The Bible—especially Colossians—tells us to do the same: "Your speech should always be pleasant and interesting, and you should know how to give the right answer to everyone" (4:6).

Paul wrote Colossians to help the congregation at Colossae deal with some false teachers who were trying to incorporate traditional philosophies into Christianity. These teachers wanted all Christians to be circumcized, follow the Jewish food laws, and worship angels as a requirement for salvation. Such work-righteousness, of course, denies the saving power of faith in Christ. Paul hoped, therefore, that the Colossians might "have the full wealth of assurance which true understanding brings" (2:2).

He wanted them to understand God's "rich and glorious secret which He has for all peoples. And the secret is that Christ is in you, which means that you will share in the glory of God" (1:27). Not only is this message to live in our hearts, but we are to "teach and instruct one another with all wisdom" (3:16).

This message still applies today, perhaps even more so, according to the late Francis Schaeffer. In his writings and his speeches, he always urged, "We must give honest answers to honest questions. Christianity is truth, truth that God has told us, and if it is truth it can answer questions. . . . Christianity demands that we have enough compassion to learn the questions of our generation . . . and try to answer."[1]

So often instead of studying God's Word to learn the answers, we take the easy way out. We either evade the question or avoid the questioner—or else we respond, "Take my word for it." Translated, that means, "Accept it on faith." While there are Biblical teachings that require acceptance by faith, so much of what God has done makes sense even to our human minds when we accept the premise that this is a God of unerring justice, unfathomable power, and unbounding love.

The story of the man who did not believe in the incarnation offers a good example. One stormy winter evening he was watching a flock of birds fly around his farmyard seeking shelter. Feeling sorry for them, he donned his overcoat and boots and went outside to open the barn door. The birds refused to enter, even though the man walked in and out several times as an example. Next he scattered some bread crumbs to guide them inside, but that also failed. Finally he said to himself, "If only I could become a bird, I would lead them in." In that moment, he realized why God came to earth in human form . . . to lead us to heaven since we cannot and will not find our way by ourselves.

But God did more than that! He sent His Holy Spirit to motivate us and provided His Word to teach us. If we prayerfully rely on them, we'll know those answers!

LET'S PRAY: Dear Lord, increase our faith and understanding so that we may always "give the right answer to everyone." In Jesus' name. Amen.

Work

That's Success!

S omeone has said that success is having your name in everything except the phone book.

Until recent times, most people would also agree that success can be achieved through hard work. Americans have long been known as hard-working pioneers and innovators.

Today, however, many people here and abroad are asking, "Is America's work ethic changing?" In Hungarian, the verb "Amerikazek" means to slow down or goof off. A survey by a New York management recruiting firm shows that bosses believe workers "steal" over four hours weekly by arriving late, leaving early, talking to friends during the workday, and doing personal business on company time. Investigations have turned up employees who regularly take on-the-job naps; and one often hears of new employees who tackle their job eagerly, only to be told by experienced workers to "slow down or else . . . !"

Only 23 percent of employees interviewed in a 1983 study said they work as hard as they could at their jobs. Perhaps that's why the same researchers found that the U.S. has the lowest productivity growth rate of all countries studied, and yet, they also discovered that the U.S. still has an "extremely strong work ethic."[1]

Could that work ethic be a result of America's strong Judeo-Christian influence? Certainly, the Bible supports hard work and devotion to duty. In fact, in Romans 12:11, Paul tells us, "Work hard and do not be lazy." Those same directions are repeated in Paul's letters to the Thessalonians.

We are introduced to the church at Thessalonica in Acts 17:1-10. Paul went there with Silas and Timothy on his second missionary journey. As he talked with worshipers at the synagogue, "some of them were convinced and joined Paul and Silas; so did many of the leading women and a large group of Greeks who worshipped God" (17:4) However, the Jewish nonbelievers caused such an uproar that Paul had to leave the city.

Later Paul twice planned to return to visit the faithful there; when that proved impossible, he wrote instead. The purpose of his first letter is to answer their questions and to encourage them.

After commending them for their love of fellow believers, Paul urges them to do even more: "Make it your aim to live a quiet life, to mind your own business and to earn your own living" (4:11). He then explains why: "In this way you will win the respect of those who are not believers, and you will not have to depend on anyone for what you need" (4:12). As always, his concern is for the spread of the Gospel!

By the time Paul wrote his second letter to them, a new problem had developed. In their enthusiastic longing for the Second Coming of the Lord, some were neglecting their business, assuming that there was no reason to work in a world which would soon end.

Paul has strong words for those who are idle for any reason: "We command these people and warn them to lead orderly lives and work to earn their own living" (3:12). He reminds them that he has always worked for everything he received; he did this as an example for them. In fact, when he was with them, he told them, "Whoever refuses to work is not allowed to eat" (3:10).

Even the Lord worked. Genesis 2:2 describes his creation of the world as "work" from which He rested on the seventh day.

For women throughout history, both in Bible times and today, work has been a way of life. The Israelite woman was expected to carry the water for the family, grind the grain, make the bread, fuel the oven, clean the house, make the clothing, care for the children, and help with the harvest! Today, more than half of American women work outside the home, then spend an average of 4.8 hours daily in homemaking. That's a total of 2.2 hours more per day working than the husband spends on family chores and his job, according to studies conducted by a sociologist.

But work has its satisfactions, whether it's a product produced or a service performed—or simply a labor of love. The joy of a job well done can make the difference between living and existing. It is only when we lovingly serve that we really live. Constant idleness may sound great when we're tired, but it's unfulfilling when we're rested. Without a job to perform, without the knowledge that we are needed, without the assurance that what we do matters, we may feel as lost as the child who prayed, "If I should die before I live . . . ."

Thanks to our Lord and Savior, we shall live after we die, and our deeds will go on living, too, in those whose lives we have touched here on earth. If they're good deeds, that's real success!

LET'S PRAY: Dear Lord, thank You for the blessing of work. Help those who have no jobs find employment so that all may know the joy of a life animated by service to You and Your creation. In Jesus' name. Amen.

Christian Homes

We Grandmother You!

"*O*ver the river and through the woods
To Grandmother's house we go . . ."
What sort of memories does that song evoke for you? Perhaps none if you're too young to have ridden a horse-drawn sleigh. Perhaps for you the verse would have more meaning if the song said:

"Aboard the airplane and through the skies"; or
"Cruising the highway in our new car
To Grandmother's condo we go . . ."

However you get there, a visit to Grandmother's home is special. That's undoubtedly why a national restaurant chain has adopted the theme: "We don't just mother you—we grandmother you!"

Speaking of his mother-in-law's love for his son, a father wrote in a national magazine recently, "I have never seen anyone love another human being so purely and without hesitation or question or doubt, a love that seems ever-deepening and enriching."[1]

Timothy too was blessed not only with a loving mother, Eunice, but also with a devout grandmother, Lois. In his Second Letter to Timothy, Paul says, "I have been reminded of your sincere faith, which first lived in your grandmother Lois and in your mother Eunice and, I am persuaded, now lives in you also" (1:5 NIV).

The two of them shared their faith with Timothy. Paul testifies to this fact when he says, "You know who your teachers were, and you remember that ever since you were a child, you have known the Holy Scriptures" (2 Tim. 3:14-15). Timothy's life demonstrates the truth of Proverbs 22:6: "Teach a child how he should live, and he will remember it all his life."

When he was an adult, Timothy was converted to Christianity by Paul, who regarded Timothy as his son in the faith. Timothy assisted Paul in his work and traveled with him on some of his missionary journeys. The two Biblical letters bearing his name were written by Paul to instruct Timothy regarding church organization and policy and his personal faith.

In the letters, Paul emphasizes that women are to dress modestly and adorn themselves with good works. In contrast to his earlier examples of Priscilla (who taught Apollos), Phoebe (a "diakonos" whom the Romans are asked to assist as she requests), and the women whom he identifies as "co-laborers," Paul here says women are not to teach men or "usurp authority" over them, and they are to be silent in church.

Most Christian churches today interpret these words in one of two ways: (1) they understand this to mean that women are not to serve as pastors; or (2) they believe this directive applied to Timothy's day and age when women were usually uneducated and could have contributed little to the teaching and discussions that were a large part of the early Christian church's worship services.

Paul also gives Timothy extensive directions regarding widows. Relatives are to respect older widows and take care of them, but Paul suggests that younger widows should remarry so that the enemy has no opportunity for speaking evil of them (see 1 Tim. 5:15). Lacking enough to do, some of the younger widows were becoming busybodies and gossips and turning away from Christ.

Someone has said that Paul was a man with "tunnel vision." Intent on sharing the Good News of Jesus Christ, he wanted Christians to be models of decorum, upholding all the customs of the day so that nothing would detract or distract from the message of the Savior.

May that also be our goal! May we nurture our children in God's Word, like Eunice and Lois—and may we "grandmother" the unchurched and the needy so that we will be channels of God's love to all whose lives we touch.

LET'S PRAY: Dear Lord, we want to be co-laborers with all who share the Gospel today. Deepen our knowledge of Your Word so that we may share Your teachings whenever the occasion arises, and especially with our children and grandchildren and other family members. Give us opportunities to serve others so that we may adorn ourselves with good works and be models of Christian love. In Jesus' name. Amen.

Self-control

They're Acting Like Children!

Enroute to catch a plane, a mother and daughter were driving along a six-lane highway. As a stoplight turned red, two cars in front of them had a minor fender-bender. A fistfight developed when the two angry drivers (one black and one white) got out of their vehicles to inspect the damage. Soon other drivers jumped out to intervene on behalf of the person of their race. Before long, nearly 40 men were battling in the median strip, and their driverless cars presented an effective roadblock.

Clenching her hands, the daughter shouted in frustration: "I have a plane to catch, and they're acting like children!"

Adults often fail to act like adults when it comes to anger, appetite, alcohol, and dozens of other stresses of modern living that require self-control. Moreover, magazine ads and newspaper articles encourage emotional behaviors. "Are you ready to indulge yourself?" asks one ad. "Women Told to Vent Anger" says a headline.

Obviously, there is a time for righteous anger. Christ was extremely upset when He drove the moneychangers from the temple. Under normal circumstances, however, Christians must strive for self-control says Paul in his Letter to Titus.

Tactful Titus was placed in Crete to establish order in the Christian community there. An argumentative group, the people of Crete were known for tilting the truth. In fact, one Bible commentary says that "the Greeks coined a special verb for lying —'to Cretize.' And it is plain from Paul's letter that even the Christians were an unruly, hot-headed, volatile bunch who needed firm handling."[1]

Therefore, Paul emphasizes that church leaders must be "self-controlled, upright, holy and disciplined" (Titus 1:8 NIV). Older women also are to be self-controlled and pure "in order to train the younger women to love their husbands and children" (2:4).

The same directive is given to all believers: "Show a gentle attitude toward everyone" (3:2). We are to do good deeds and "avoid stupid arguments, long lists of ancestors, quarrels, and fights about the Law" (3:9). The reason, of course, is "so that no one will speak evil of the message that comes from God" (2:5).

Paul's Letter to Philemon offers a good example of how followers of Christ are expected to demonstrate self-control. Actually the letter is addressed not just to Philemon but also to his wife, Apphia, and their son, Archippus. Apphia is the only woman to whom a letter of Scripture is specifically directed by name.

Paul wants them to welcome Onesimus, their runaway slave, back as a brother in Christ. This will require much self-control since Onesimus most likely took some money or household items with him when he left Philemon's home in Colossae. Onesimus traveled to Rome where he somehow came in contact with Paul, who was in prison there. Under Paul's influence, Onesimus became a Christian. Paul, the "spiritual father," views the slave as "my own son in Christ" (10). Realizing, though, that Onesimus must return to Philemon, Paul writes to the family, urging them to "welcome him back just as you would welcome me" (17).

That's asking a lot! Sometimes the Lord asks a lot of us, too, but rarely as much as He required of Paul, who endured beatings, mob action, insults, misunderstandings, desertion, and eventually death because of his faith. Throughout it all Paul eagerly awaited "the prize of victory awarded for a righteous life, the prize which the Lord, the righteous Judge, will give me on that Day—and not only to me, but to all those who wait with love for him to appear" (2 Tim. 4:8).

That's our reassurrance too when life is difficult and it seems the Lord has given us more than we can bear. At such times, we can rely on the Lord's promises that He knows our needs and will provide. As the song says, "Yesterday He died for me. . . . Today He lives for me. . . . Tomorrow He comes for me. . . . Jesus Christ the Lord!"*

LET'S PRAY: Thank You, Lord, for dwelling in us so that we never have to face any struggle alone. Help us to have the confidence and self-control of Paul so that we, too, may say when our last day on earth comes, "I have done my best in the race, I have run the full distance, and I have kept the faith" (2 Tim. 4:7). In Jesus' name. Amen.

---

*"Yesterday, Today and Tomorrow." © Copyright 1966 by Singspirations Music/ASCAP. All rights reserved. International copyright secured. Used by permission of the Zondervan Music Group, Nashville, Tenn.

Peace

The Unaccepted Gift

When a company inadvertently failed to fill an order for two months, the angered customer asked for her money back. The company sent the refund immediately, enclosing it with a letter of apology and a gift to make amends. The customer refused to accept the package. "I don't want it!" she told the postman. Then she wrote another letter to the company, complaining because her check had not arrived.

Sometimes we refuse to accept the Lord's gifts, too—like His gift of peace. "Peace is what I leave with you; it is my own peace that I give you," He says (John 14:27). Our response is like that of the woman who went to the doctor and said, "Give me something to make me better without my having to give up any of the foods that made me ill."

We want peace in the world without giving up the economic benefits of war. We want peace of mind without placing our lives in the Lord's hands. We want peace with God without repentance.

Actually *repentance* is the key to every kind of peace, but how difficult it is to say, "I'm sorry," on either the international or the personal level. One mother found a solution by putting up a blackboard. When any of her three children had disagreements and afterwards did not want to face the sibling they had wronged, they were allowed to write their apology on the blackboard. In life, it's not that easy.

In his book *God's Way Out of Futility* Richard C. Halverson says, "Some love Jesus little because they have been forgiven little; not because they do not need forgiveness, but they would rather endure guilt, try to cover it, than walk in the light, acknowledge their sin, and receive the forgiveness and cleansing of God. They love little because they have been forgiven little."[1]

Peace is the result of forgiveness, and forgiveness comes only after repentance. Repentance is more than saying, "I'm sorry." It includes a resolve to turn away from our sin and follow the Lord's will. Or, as the author of the Letter to the Hebrews says, "Try to be at peace with everyone, and try to live a holy life" (12:14).

The letter was written to encourage a group of Jewish Christians who were being persecuted by their neighbors and were in danger of falling away from their faith. Today's English Bibles generally attribute the letter to Paul, but there has been debate about this over the years. Luther believed Apollos may have written it.

Regardless of who the author is, the Book of Hebrews does a masterful job of stressing the strengths of the Christian faith. Jesus is greater than Moses and greater than the angels, says the writer. Christ guarantees a better covenant; He serves as our high priest in heaven, which is a better country than any on earth. God's New Testament plan is better than His Old Testament law. In short: in Christ, we have the best there is!

That alone should give us peace of mind! Therefore, says the writer, let's be thankful, and "let's worship God in a way that will please Him" (12:28).

Despite His desire for us to live in peace, the Lord predicts that there will always be wars and rumors of war. (How well He knows us!) "Countries will fight each other; kingdoms will attack one another," He says in Matthew (24:7).

Certainly, that's still true today despite all the secular and religious efforts over the centuries to establish world peace. Encyclopedia listings of peace-keeping organizations and peaceful periods in history are short. They include the Pax Romana, which preserved peace in the Roman Empire from 27 B.C. to A.D. 180; the "Truce of God," announced by clergy in the Middle Ages, which forbade fighting on Sundays and holy days; the

Hague Conferences of 1899 and 1907 to seek international peace through arms limitations; the League of Nations; and the United Nations.

Their failures leave Christians with a challenge: to share the peace of Christ so extensively and so lovingly that His will may be done by everyone on earth. Or, as the writer to the Hebrews says, "May the God of peace provide you with every good thing you need in order to do His will, and may He, through Jesus Christ, do in us what pleases Him. And to Christ be the glory forever and ever! Amen" (13:21).

LET'S PRAY: Dearest Jesus, we accept Your gift of peace. Enable us to share it with the entire world . . . to Your glory forever and ever. Amen.

Neighbors

Friends—or Strangers?

Quilting bees, barn raisings, threshing bees, west-ward-moving wagon trains—American history is filled with examples of neighbors helping neighbors. In those difficult times, few things were done alone.

Ironically, as the population has mushroomed, the lives of many Americans have become more isolated. Today it's possible to live in an apartment building for years and not know your neighbors. In fact, with the security system in metropolitan high-rise apartments, it's even possible to be a recluse in the midst of thousands of people. The prevailing attitude is: "Don't bother me; I don't want to get involved." As a result, people can be robbed and sometimes murdered in a crowd or near their own home in broad daylight, and no one will come to their assistance.

James would be appalled!

The Book of James is the first of seven general letters in the Bible. Written to all Christians, it deals with the temptation of "cheap grace." Since Christ died for us, since we have forgiveness of sins by grace through faith in Him, does it really matter how we live? "YES," says James emphatically, "it does!"

Faith without action is dead. It is not true faith, he says, for true faith shows itself in action. Or in his words: "What good is it for someone to say that he has faith if his actions do not prove it? Can that faith save him? Suppose there are brothers or sisters who need clothes and don't have enough to eat. What good is there in your saying to them, 'God bless you! Keep warm and eat well!'—if you don't give them the necessities of life? So it is with faith: if it is alone and includes no actions, then it is dead" (2:14-17).

Faith is made complete through our actions, James explains (2:22), and as an example, he cites Rahab: "Was not even Rahab the prostitute considered righteous for what she did when she gave lodging to the spies and sent them off in a different direction? (2:25 NIV).

The guideline, says James, is: "Love your neighbor as you love yourself" (2:8).That's exactly what Christ told the teacher of the Law who tried to trap Him in Luke 10. "Who is my neighbor?" the man asked. Jesus responded with the parable of the Good Samaritan. Our neighbor is everyone we meet.

Today our neighborhood has expanded. As the world shrinks through TV and satellites, we have opportunities to be Good Samaritans not only to those in our local community but also to the orphans of the Orient, the starving of Africa, and the handicapped and homeless around the globe.

Our Lord gives further guidelines for neighborliness in the Ten Commandments. Perhaps the one we break most easily is the eighth (Do not bear false witness against your neighbor). James compares the power of the tongue with a tiny flame that destroys a large forest, or a rudder that steers a large ship. We can tame wild animals, but not our tongue, he says.

How true that is! We leave church on Sunday complaining that the organ was too loud, the soloist too shrill, and the sermon too long. James says, "Do not criticize one another" (4:11), and Paul says, "Do good to everyone, and especially to those who belong to our family in the faith" (Gal. 6:10).

We indulge in criticism to boost our sense of self-worth. By pushing down another person, another nationality, or another creed through gossip, slander, and insult, we strive to elevate our own image in the eyes of others and assure ourselves that we are worth loving. "I'm better than she is," we imply.

Christ's method is different: "Humble yourselves before the Lord, and He will lift you up" (4:10). That's a lot easier—and a lot more permanent!

Moreover, through Christ we are made friends with the Lord. As 2 Corinthians 5:17-18 says: "When anyone is joined to Christ, he is a new being. . . . All this is done by God, who through Christ changed us from enemies into his friends and gave us the task of making others his friends also." That includes our neighbors.

LET'S PRAY: Dear Lord, teach us to "do unto others as we would have them do unto us." Break down the high-rise barriers of our heart so that our faith too can be made complete through action, and through that action, cause our neighbors to want to become our friends—and Yours also. In Jesus' name. Amen.

Gifts

Decisions, Decisions!

Dressed in sloppy slacks, a torn, dirty blouse, and wearing long, scraggly hair, a young woman was shopping for a birthday present for a friend. After finding just the right gift, the young woman carefully selected just the right wrapping paper and ribbon. "I want it to look nice," she told the clerk.

Relating the experience later to her own family, the clerk said, "How I wish she would gift wrap herself, too!"

Each of us *is* a gift. James tells us that "every good gift and every perfect present comes from heaven; it comes down from God, the Creator of heavenly lights .... By His own will He brought us into being through the word of truth, so that we should have first place among all His creatures" (1:17-18).

At a churchwomen's Christmas party, the committee provided gift tags to be used as name tags. "What you are is God's gift to you," they said. "What you do with your life is your gift to God."

That sometimes presents a problem—deciding what to do with our lives. We want everything to be perfect—like the pictures painted by artists in the Middle Ages. Most religious figures then were portrayed with halos and wings. After the Renaissance and the Reformation, the style changed to realism. Then the artists showed people with smudges on their clothes and dirt on their feet. The message was: it's O.K. to be ourselves. God loves us, dirty feet and all.

Nevertheless, decisions relating to our life are difficult to make. We face so many fears and roadblocks:

1. *Fear of failure.* If we make the wrong decision, it hurts our pride.

2. *Fear of change.* We are all creatures of habit.

3. *Fear of criticism.* We want people to like us.

4. *So many choices.* Life today is a supermarket of options. Unlike the days when cornflakes were the only cold breakfast cereal, every morning requires dozens of choices.

5. *Lack of goals.* "I don't know what I want to be," many worried college freshmen admit.

6. *Failure to understand ourselves.* Many of us do not know who we are. We're like the cat that regularly disappeared from home for two or three days each week. After one absence, she returned wearing a new collar. Puzzled, the owners placed a tag on the collar: "My name is Spot. I live at 202 S. Jackson St." When the cat returned the next time, a new tag said, "At 12 Northview Rd., I'm known as Princess." Perhaps you're thinking, "Lucky cat—she has the best of both worlds." Actually, she's to be pitied, for she doesn't know who she is.

As Christians, we do know who we are: we are God's creation, and we are His redeemed children. That gives us real worth. That means we can accept ourselves because God has accepted us. He not only made us—He declared our personal worth at Calvary.

What a great and generous God! As James says, "God gives generously and graciously to all" (1:5). To each of us He gives gifts so that we can be a gift—and if we err in our efforts, repentance always brings forgiveness. That means we don't have to worry about failure. The only real failure is failure to reach as high as we can.

That requires planning. As our mothers used to say, "If you fail to plan, you plan to fail; so plan your work, then work your plan."

How? Begin with prayer, opening the doors to God's guidance. Next analyze your talents. If you can't carry a tune, it's foolish to aim at musical stardom just because you have a loud voice. Finally, make a decision and get to work!

According to James, if we are guided by the wisdom

of God, we will be peaceful, gentle, and friendly (3:17), and we can expect a harvest of good deeds. Who could ask for more?

LET'S PRAY: Dear Lord, You have made us what we are, and You have given us the greatest gift there is: salvation through faith in our loving Savior, Your only Son, our Lord. We praise and thank You, and in gratitude we offer our lives in service to You. In Jesus' name. Amen.

Ageless Beauty

Insured but Sure to Disappear

S he does no housework; it might damage her hands. They are insured for thousands of dollars because she is a hands model. When you see a hand displaying diamond rings, a rare broach, or an expensive wristwatch in a TV commercial or magazine ad, it may be hers. The skin is smooth, the nails perfectly manicured. No blemish is visible.

Beauty—and the maintenance of it—has become a billion dollar business today. A cosmetic manufacturer offers 154 shades of lipstick that represent "the difference between looking good and looking great." Another markets "a corrective cream for lips." A hair coloring product promises to give you confidence, and a hair masque "turns strands of hair into streams of glistening light."

The women of Bible times would have been just as interested in such products as we are today. From Isaiah, we learn that the women of Jerusalem used perfumes and wore ornaments on their ankles, heads, and necks. They had rings for their fingers and their noses. They enjoyed fine robes, gowns, cloaks, belts, and purses, as well as revealing garments, linen handkerchiefs, scarves, and long veils.

God's priorities are different. As Proverbs 31:30 says, "Charm is deceptive and beauty disappears, but a women who honors the Lord should be praised."

In 1 Peter, God tells women not to depend on "outward aids to make yourselves beautiful, such as the way you fix your hair, or the jewelry you put on, or the dresses you wear. Instead, your beauty should consist of your true inner self, the ageless beauty of a gentle and quiet spirit, which is of the greatest value in God's sight" (3:3-4).

The passage is reminiscent of 1 Timothy 2:9-10 where women are urged to "be modest and sensible about their clothes and to dress properly; not with fancy hair styles or with gold ornaments or pearls or expensive dresses, but with good deeds, as is proper for women who claim to be religious."

Religious women are to do good and not be afraid of anything. (1 Peter 3:6). Husbands are to "treat them with respect, because they also will receive . . . God's gift of life" (1 Peter 3:7).

Wives in turn are to submit themselves to their husbands, "so that if any of them do not believe God's word, your conduct will win them over to believe. It will not be necessary for you to say a word, because they will see how pure and reverent your conduct is (1 Peter 3:1-2)."

The *Bible Almanac* includes an old Jewish story which demonstrates the importance of the woman's role in Israel: "A pious man once married a pious woman. They were childless, so they eventually agreed to divorce one another. The husband then married a wicked woman, and she made him wicked. The pious woman married a wicked man and made him righteous. The moral of the story is that the woman sets the tone for the home.[1]

The almanac goes on to comment: "The Israelite mother held an important place in the life of the family. To a large degree, she was the key to a successful family or the cause of its failure. She could have incalculable influence on her husband and her children. Israel's history and its culture owe a great deal to these hardworking women."[2]

Certainly, such women demonstrated the ideal held up by Peter, John, and Jude in their letters: "Our love should not be just words and talk; it must be true love, which shows itself in action" (1 John 3:18). Over and over they encourage believers to love one another—and to beware of false teachers.

The early church was undergoing difficult times at this period in history. Not only were there false teachers who denied the humanity of Christ and rebelled against authority, but Nero was beginning his persecution of Christians. Eventually, even Peter was one of the casualties of the emperor's vengeful purge.

Tradition says that after years of teaching and preaching, accompanied in his travels by his wife, Peter was crucified in Rome. Because he did not think himself worthy of being crucified in the same manner as Christ, he asked to be placed on the cross head downward.

It is therefore appropriate that Peter also deals with Christian suffering in his first letter. He says that believers should be glad, not sad or ashamed, when they are chosen to share Christ's sufferings. For Christ, suffering was a prelude to glory, and it is the same for His followers.

When God called us, He promised us a blessing, and as Peter reminds us, He always keeps His promise (2 Peter 3:9). That blessing is a home in heaven, and that's worth more than any earthly beauty or benefit. It requires no insurance policy to protect it, for faith in Christ gives us all the assurance that's needed.

LET'S PRAY: Thank You, Lord, for making faith in You, and not physical beauty, the criterion for heaven. Thank You for giving Your life so that we can be assured of a home with You forever. We trust in Your promise to never give us more than we can bear. Watch over us during our lifetime, and let Your kingdom come soon. In Jesus' name. Amen.

Heaven

The Bride of Christ

*H*ow's your day been so far? If you're like the young mother whose children spilled a bottle of black liquid shoe polish on the new living room carpet, your answer may be, "Horrible!" Or imagine the frustration of a young professional woman who dropped a can of cherry soda at the office, only to have the top burst open and the contents spray all over her face and her expensive new suit!

Each of us can add our daily tales of woe: the car broke down on the expressway during the rush hour, dinner burned in the oven, our dog bit the neighbor . . . yes, each of us regularly has experiences we'd rather forget.

Few of our problems, however, match those of the early Christians. Not only were false teachers splintering the Christian communities, but the believers were being harassed from outside the church by both Jews and Gentiles. Many of the faithful were facing persecution, possible imprisonment, and even death.

Some were becoming depressed and falling away from the faith. John, exiled on the island of Patmos, wrote the Book of Revelation to encourage the faithful by sharing a series of visions.

"God is in control, no matter how things may look," John assures them and us. "Christ, not the emperor, is Lord of history. He has the key of destiny itself. And He *is* coming again to execute justice. There is a glorious, wonderful future for every faithful believer—and especially for those who lay down their lives for Christ. This world and all that happens in it is in God's hands. His love and care for His people are unfailing."[1]

Writing in the apocalyptic style that was popular

then, John uses pictures, symbols, colors, and numbers to make his point. His readers most likely understood his abstractions and allegories, but many of them are confusing to us. Even Luther said, "My spirit cannot adapt itself to this book."[2]

Nevertheless, Revelation is filled with hope and encouragement even for the casual reader. As we see the Lord's promises to His people, His ultimate conquest over evil, the beautiful descriptions of the wedding of the Lamb, and the glorious picture of heaven, we can rise above the problems of this life and each morning say with the psalmist, "This is the day the Lord has made; let us rejoice and be glad in it" (118:24 NIV). All our earthly struggles fade into unimportance as we contemplate the future of the faithful with the Lord.

Often in John's visions, a woman symbolizes a special truth or plan of God. In chapter 12:1, a woman "whose dress was the sun and who had the moon under her feet and a crown of twelve stars on her head" represents God's people. The passage describes God's loving provision of a Savior and His protection of the faithful. When pursued by Satan, the woman is "given the two wings of a large eagle in order to fly to her place in the desert, where she will be taken care of" in safety (12:14).

The joy of the wedding day is the basis for two other comparisons. In chapter 19:7-8, John hears a crowd, like a roaring waterfall, say: "Let us rejoice and be glad; let us praise His greatness! For the time has come for the wedding of the Lamb, and His bride has prepared herself for it. She has been given clean, shining linen to wear. (The linen is the good deeds of God's people.)" Surely there is no wedding dress more beautiful for the church of Christ.

In chapter 21, heaven is compared with "a bride dressed to meet her husband." The Spirit takes control of John and carries him to the top of a high mountain to see heaven, "the Bride, the wife of the Lamb" (21:9)—and what a radiant sight he beholds! How difficult it is to wait to see it ourselves—the angels and all the saints, including our departed loved ones; the city made of crystal-clear gold, with a foundation of topaz, sapphire, and other precious stones; the gates of pearl; the walls of jasper; and above all, at last to see the Lord!

John tells us: "The Spirit and the Bride say, 'Come!' . . . Come whoever is thirsty; accept the water of life as a gift, whoever wants it" (22:17).

Oh, Lord, we *do* want it—so come!

LET'S PRAY: Dear Lord, how grateful we are for Your Holy Word, especially for Revelation and its glimpse of our heavenly home. How we long to be there with You, but until that day, keep us faithful and clothe us with good deeds that radiate Your love to others. In Jesus' name. Amen.

In Conclusion

Rejoice

A girl, studying her lines for the Sunday school Christmas program, was having difficulty memorizing the unfamiliar words in her verse: "And behold, I bring you glad tidings of great joy."

"What does 'tidings' mean?" she asked her mother.

"It means 'good news,' " the mother responded.

Facing the packed church the night of the program, the girl became frightened and again forgot her lines. She stammered for a moment and then blurted out: "Hey, I've got good news for you!"

We have Good News, too! It's there for us in God's Word. It's there for women—as we have seen during our walk from Genesis through Revelation:

Good News of a GREAT GOD who loved us enough to send His only Son to save us;

Good News of FORGIVENESS of sins by grace through FAITH, rather than the uncertainty of salvation through works;

Good News of a beautiful HEAVENLY HOME that awaits all of us who believe; and

Good News that causes us to REJOICE, because the Bible makes it obvious that the Lord cares for you and me as individuals.

How exciting it has been to read the true stories of real people—real men and women, who faced danger and hardship with courage and were blessed because of their trust in the Lord.

In these devotions, we've become better acquainted with our Lord and with many of the Biblical women—women like Mary, Deborah, Dorcas, Phoebe, Priscilla, and Huldah, to mention just a few. But there are still others we haven't discussed. For instance, we think of the following:

The Syrophoenician woman who begged the Lord to cast the unclean spirit out of her daughter. Because of the woman's faith and her humility (she was willing to accept just the crumbs of the Lord's blessing), her request was granted (Matt. 15:21-28).

The woman who was criticized by others but won the Lord's praise when she washed His feet with her tears and poured perfume on them (Luke 7:36-50).

The adulteress whom Jesus saved when others wanted to stone her to death, while making no mention of the man involved (John 8:1-11).

The women, like Hagar and Manoah's wife (Samson's mother), to whom the Angel of the Lord appeared with help and encouragement (Gen. 16; 21; Judges 13).

Mary Magdalene, Joanna, and Susanna, who supported Christ and His disciples with their resources (Luke 8:1-3).

Elizabeth and Jochebed and Anna and Hannah and the lame woman who was healed.

And yes, the list goes on. And each has a message for us. One lesson in particular we must not overlook—that of Sarah and Hagar. For years, Sarah and her maid Hagar, who came with her from Egypt, were good friends. Jealousy developed, however, after Hagar gave birth to a child—jealousy so bitter that Hagar first ran away and later was forced to flee permanently.

Too often today we see that same type of jealousy and bitterness surfacing between women who work outside the home and those who concentrate on homemaking and motherhood, between women who join churchwomen's organizations and those who prefer to serve the parish in other ways, and between women in competitive roles of all sorts. Yet in Christ we are all one; we are all part of the same body, with our Savior as the Head.

Through Him, we each are given different talents and different ways of serving—for the good of the whole body, for the blessing of all believers. Let's rejoice in His gifts, rejoice in our likenesses *and* our differences, rejoice in the great opportunities that we have to serve today, rejoice in the encouragement God's Word offers to us as women, and then *together* move forward to praise His Name and share His Good News, each in our own God-appointed way.

Notes

The Value of Life: I'm So Glad I'm Me!
(Exodus)

1. Dr. Bruch is with Southbury Training School in Connecticut.

Blessings of the Law: Choose Life!
(Deuteronomy)

1. Dick Hyman, "The Trenton Pickle Ordinance and Other Bonehead Legislation," (Brattleboro, Vt.: Stephen Greene Press, 1976).

Prayer: Praying Is Believing
(Joshua)

1. Ruth Fritz Meyer, *Women on a Mission* (St. Louis: Concordia, 1967), p. 48.

True Love: No Wonder All Women Love You!
(Ecclesiastes/Song of Solomon)

1. *Eerdmans' Handbook to the Bible* (Grand Rapids: Eerdmans, 1973), p. 367.

Trust: No One Told the Neighbors
(Luke)

1. See Luke 1:75.

Bible Study: Letter from the Lord
(Luke)

1. See Jer. 23:29; Heb. 5:12-14; Ps. 119:105; Heb. 4:12; James 1:23-25; Acts 20:32.

The Trinity: Three-in-One—the Total God
(Luke)

1. *Eerdmans' Handbook,* p. 514.

2. Martin Luther quoted by Paul E. Kretzmann, *Popular Com-*

mentary of the Bible: The New Testament, Vol. 1 (St. Louis: Concordia, 1921), p. 259.

3. Kretzmann, p. 348.

Careers: Profits Doubled
(Acts)

1. Elaine Weiss, "Big Deals," *Savvy,* May 1985.

Christian Service: Strengthen One Another
(Romans)

1. Martin Luther quoted by Paul E. Kretzmann, *Popular Commentary of the Bible: The New Testament,* Vol. 2 (St. Louis: Concordia, 1921), p. 2.

Marriage: Submit Yourselves to One Another
(Ephesians)

1. *Marriage Encounter Magazine,* 13, No. 5 (June 1984), p. 12.

Unity: Dealing with Differences Differently
(Philippians)

1. Francis A. Schaeffer, *The Mark of the Christian* (Downers Grove, Ill.: InterVarsity Press, 1970), p. 30.

2. Schaeffer, pp. 30-31.

Understanding: Give an Answer!
(Colossians)

1. "Let the Earth Hear His Voice," (Minneapolis: World Wide Publications), p. 373.

Work: That's Success
(1 and 2 Thessalonians)

1. Daniel Yankelovich and John Immerwahr, "The World at Work," 1984; reported in the *Milwaukee Journal,* July 28, 1985.

Christian Homes: We Grandmother You!
(1 and 2 Timothy)

1. Robert Brody, "She's a Fulltime GRANDMOTHER," *50 Plus,* November 1985, p. 20.

Self-control: They're Acting Like Children!
(Titus/Philemon)

1. *Eerdmans' Handbook,* p. 623.

Peace: The Unaccepted Gift
(Hebrews)

1. Richard C. Halverson, *God's Way Out of Futility* (Grand Rapids: Zondervan), p. 106.

Ageless Beauty: Insured but Sure to Disappear
(1 and 2 Peter/1, 2, 3 John/Jude)

1. Packer, Tenney, and White, *The Bible Almanac* (Thomas Nelson Publishers, 1980), p. 430.

2. *Bible Almanac,* p. 430.

Heaven: The Bride of Christ
(Revelation)

1. *Eerdmans' Handbook,* p. 645.

2. Walter R. Roehrs and Martin H. Franzmann, *Concordia Self-Study Commentary* (St. Louis: Concordia, 1979), p. 285.

Taege, Marlys
AUTHOR

Women throug the Bible
TITLE
(devotions for women's groups)

DATE DUE	BORROWER'S NAME